THE ART OF WAR

THE ART OF WAR

*From the Age of Napoleon
to the Present Day*

By Cyril Falls

A HESPERIDES BOOK

NEW YORK • OXFORD UNIVERSITY PRESS

1961

© Oxford University Press 1961
First published as a Hesperides Book, 1961
Second Printing, 1962

PRINTED IN THE UNITED STATES OF AMERICA

Der Krieg ist offenbar eine Kunst und keine Wissenschaft, eine Kunst, bei welcher das Sublime wie bei allen Künsten nicht gelehrt werden kann.—FIELD MARSHAL RADETZKY

War is manifestly an art and not a science, an art by which, as is true of all arts, the sublime cannot be taught.

PREFATORY NOTE

THE period covered by this book is from Napoleon to our own times. It is in no sense a military history of that period. It is, in short, an analysis. Its object is to show how land armies, navies, and in the final phase air forces, were handled: that is, leadership, training, strategy, tactics, equipment, and weapons. Attention is given to theory, but in terms as simple as can be found; without this it would not be possible to show what governments, their ministries concerned with war and defence, and their higher commands were trying to do or how their ideas evolved as the material at their disposal developed.

It is hoped that a short book of this type will meet a need. The type is much rarer, especially in this country, than military history. The majority of the works on tactics deal with much shorter periods, some of them only with the tactics of a single brief war, the Franco-German War of 1870, for example. Many general readers do not want such detail or want it only rarely, to bring out some valuable point, and would find a great deal presented in these treatises repellent. As for the big works devoted to both strategy and tactics—Jomini, Clausewitz, Hamley, Foch—they exercise a strange fascination but upon strictly limited numbers only. Readers who feel inclined to tackle any of them can do so and are recommended to try their teeth on Clausewitz, the genius of the group, even though toothache may be the result.

One cannot study war with any benefit to oneself or to others for as many years as I have without producing some ideas original in greater or lesser degree, though certain of them may be unsound. Equally, one cannot go far in writing a book on the subject without using the ideas of those who have trodden these paths already. Here quotations are short and are followed by notes showing their origins, as are striking facts not given as quotations. I consider therefore that in the prefatory note only one acknowledgement by name is called for. It is to Herr Oskar Regele, whose biography, *Feldmarschall Radetzky*, is unique in the information it gives of this remarkable soldier. The lapidary quality of the words quoted at the beginning of my book will suggest, what is indeed the case, that the old man was almost as good with a pen as with a sword.

CONTENTS

LIST OF DIAGRAMS

INTRODUCTORY

WAR is a feature of human behaviour. From the earliest groping attempts to organize society, from the most primitive communities, we see through history disputes decided, the goods of tribes seized and defended, by force of arms, by war. Man has always lived under the threat of death, wounds, subjection, starvation, and impoverishment at the hands of his kind. The cruelty and suffering imposed by war upon mankind, whenever we reflect upon it, causes us astonishment that creatures out of the same mould should behave in this way. The fact remains that they have found themselves unable to devise any other means of reaching their ends. At first no other occurred to them; war was a matter of course. Later on they propounded and tried to put into effect measures to prevent war or at least render it less likely: treaties, leagues, resort to arbitration, pledges of absolute renunciation. These efforts proved vain; even though decision by arms ceased to be automatic, war remained the ultimate resort. Its profit and loss account, over-weighted though it is on the debit side, includes also credit entries, moral as well as material, notably in wars of liberation or for the defence of freedom.

The English historians of the late nineteenth and early twentieth centuries were revolted by the brutality and irrationality of war. Their aversion to it led them into puerile attempts to minimize its importance and refusal to concern themselves with it. Seldom can a famous historian have committed himself to a judgement more fallacious than that of John Richard Green: 'War plays a small part in the real story of European nations, and in that of England its part is smaller than in any.'

In fact, the history of mankind has been profoundly influenced by war. This influence extends from the fate of nations, whose very existence is sometimes created or ended by it, down to the fate of the humblest individuals, their welfare, surroundings, and status in society. It spreads into literature, music, painting, sculpture, architecture, science, medicine, and surgery. War pervades languages, so that speech and writing are reinforced by a host of bellicose terms, phrases, and metaphors. And the part played by war in the 'real story of England', of the United Kingdom, and the British Government has actually been immense. To consider only the experience open to Green when he wrote in 1874, the struggles with the Spain of Phillip II and the France of Louis XIV and Napoleon were matters of life and death. It is distortion of history to pretend that this was not the case. The extent of the damage done by a lost war, an invasion, or a military occupation is another matter. It often proves to be smaller than is believed at the moment. The clouds of depression and shame may blow over surprisingly soon.

The fallacy outlined above—which is in any case becoming less general—is perhaps less to be condemned than another, sometimes proceeding from the same writers. It is that wars are purely aberrations and for the most part due to the wickedness of sovereigns and politicians who force or entice their peoples into them. Dynastic wars have indeed been common and princes have led subjects to war for provinces, the acquisition of which has done no good to any man or any institution except the royal personage and his treasury. Politicians have brought on wars the significance of which no one but themselves has fully understood. Yet these have been, even before the Napoleonic age, by no means the only types of war.

Indeed, while the term 'economic war' takes on a modern look, this is only because economic studies are modern. The earliest kinds of war were purely economic, battles for hunting grounds. Next came struggles for pasture; then for land tilled or fit for tillage. They originated fierce and terrible wars. In the wilder and darker regions of the European and Asiatic mass, land hunger set in motion vast waves of savage, vigorous, peoples, waves that rolled into and through the settled and civilized lands to reach the shores of the Mediterranean and the Atlantic. In this great folk movement one race after another, pushed out of its own lands, strove to possess itself of others in order to support life. It was a tremendous heaving of populations. We have seen the like in our own times. We speak of it as 'pressure of population on the means of subsistence'. It has been exemplified in Japan—where, let us note, it still exists. The immediate cause of the Japanese attack on Pearl Harbour was the megalomania of an all-powerful military clique, but it was rooted in Japan's annexation of Manchuria and her grip on Chinese ports, finance, and trade, and these in turn were due to land hunger. It may well be that this cause—call it 'hunger' in one word because it amounts to that or to dread of it—has from first to last been the most potent of all causes of war.

Another is fanatical frenzy. This has often accompanied dynastic wars. Sometimes it has prevented their settlement when kings or governments would have been content to wind them up. It has proved most unrelenting and cruel in conflicts of a special kind, wars of religion. We know, of course, that the most famous war of this type in modern times, the Thirty Years War in the seventeenth century, was in part caused and kept going by political ambitions and intrigue. We are grateful to the historians who continue to add to our knowledge of these factors, but we should beware of following them if the writers go on to belittle religious fervour. Surely this is the feature which made the conduct of these wars so revolting.

Alas! the promise of the cool, sceptical, and moderate eighteeenth century that, whatever might be the future of warfare, this element would no longer intrude, has not been fulfilled. We have found to our cost that it can intrude, and now see material for another 'ideological war' lying about. This, however, is created by different forms of religion: not faith in supernatural powers such as made Moslem fight Christian and Protestant fight Catholic, but conflicts of material philosophies. And because one of these creeds or ideologies, Russian Communism, has proclaimed its intention of dominating the world, it breeds antagonism potentially stronger even than that which bred the Thirty Years War.

Hatred and bigotry in popular masses have long been, in one form or another, one of the greatest perils to peace. They are so still. Whether or not war can be eradicated, it is a deep-seated instinct or, if you like, malady.

Of late there has developed a widespread conviction that the appalling power of the weapons with which science has armed mankind has made their use in war increasingly improbable, and that since, as it is asserted, 'great' wars involving the deepest interests of great powers are unlikely to be fought without them, therefore great wars are unlikely to be fought at all. The argument may well be correct. We must hope it is. Yet it is to be regretted that we should have to rely on fear to save us from war, rather than virtue or even a combination of virtue and fear. Virtue would be a stronger guarantee, and if fear were to contain an admixture of virtue our generation would be provided with a moral buckler against war which it does not as a whole now possess.

It is because war is an actuality, because it has always existed and has continuously affected the destinies of mankind, that study of its history, of the causes which have produced war in the past and the means by which it has been conducted should not be treated as an abstract exercise or specialist subject. We may hope to avoid another 'great' war, but we have no positive assurance that we have put the prospect behind us. The fact that our hope of escape is founded on the terrible nature of nuclear war leaves open the risk of one side reaching the conclusion that its chance has come to destroy the other while it faces the minimum volume of retaliation it can ever hope to encounter. Moreover, small wars without nuclear weapons have not been avoided and remain a possibility.

The writer does not pretend that the subject of this book, even were it better presented than it is here, is a necessity for the lay student. His most useful plot in the field of military history may be rather the origin of wars, the reactions of nations to their threat, the way in which their characteristic strategy is moulded by political conditions, economic problems, and especially geography. The writer does claim that the subject of how wars are fought is a valuable feature of history and ought to be an interesting one. He also contends that the sense of something like guilt which attacks certain people approaching the art of war is unjustified. You are no more likely to become a militarist or a jingo through addiction to military history than an ornithologist is likely to feed his children on gobbets of raw flesh, still warm, because he has become fascinated by the behaviour of birds of prey.

War has produced many theoretical writers. On the whole they have not found the atmosphere of Britain favourable. This is perhaps mainly because Britons are suspicious of theory applied to a business as practical and at the same time as uncertain as war. Germany and France have provided most of the famous theorists. The cloudy, diffuse, and repetitive Clausewitz, master of the obvious, yet ever and anon giving out sparks of genius, is never likely to be deposed from the office of high priest in the temple of Mars.

The phrases 'art of war' and 'business of war' have just been used. They recall the fact that controversy has arisen about the definition of the conduct of war. Should we call it an art, a science, a business, or, as Field-Marshal Lord Wavell, perhaps only as a quip, suggested, a very rough game? From certain points of view all are appropriate. Jomini treated war as a matter of science and the operations of war mainly as a matter of angles, but, though he carried such ideas to the point of absurdity, he also said a good deal worth saying. From another aspect science of several sorts, engineering, mechanical, electronic, and now above all that of nuclear fission and the propulsion of long-range nuclear missiles, has played a part of ever-growing importance in the waging of war, or in equipment for it. Again, administration and logistics are today a veritable business. The movements of forces require technical skill and precision of a high order. The mere catering for their food is more difficult than the task of Messrs. Lyons, because they can estimate in advance their needs at any hour of the day, the week, and the year, and because their work is not interfered with by hostile forces. (It was interfered with during the Second World War, but not on a scale comparable to the destruction of communications and stores in the field.) And food supply in war is relatively simple because weight and bulk are roughly constant, whereas ammunitition is heavy and its consumption varies enormously. Finally, there is a certain resemblance between warfare and a rough, very rough, game of football or a boxing match. The boxer returns to his guard immediately after the delivery of a blow. Football players pack the goal when an attack has failed and the opposition seizes the initiative.

Yet the title of this book, 'The Art of War', has not been chosen at random. The intention is to study the tools and devices of leadership such as armaments, transport, manœuvre and tactics; but the primary subject is to be leadership. It is maintained that leadership is essentially an art. Even when we are considering the moral element in leadership we find that art often enters into that too. Few will disagree if they are familiar with the campaigns and personalities of leaders such as Alexander the Great, Marlborough, Napoleon, and in modern wars Allenby and Montgomery. Strategy is the *art* of conducting a campaign. Tactics is the *art* of conducting a battle or section of a battle. The role of the great commander and his ambiance, often indeed his temperament, have an affinity closer to those of the artist than to those of the scientist. For one thing, the leader is concerned with a vital element, as sensitive as a violin string and as likely to snap from wear, climate or mishandling, the morale of the men who fight under his orders. For another, certainties or near-certainties which he seizes before acting in battle are not of the nature of scientific formulae. They are sudden apprehensions; sometimes they can—though the word has become one of derision when applied to Hitler's wilder fancies—even be called 'intuitions'. So we shall be considering the art of war.

Nearly all writers on war have drawn up a list of principles. Few, and none of the wisest, pretend that they are immutable rules, still less that they will show the soldier what to do on the battlefield. It can only be said of them that they are conveniences, which some successful soldiers have never even tried to remember and have neglected without, so far as we can tell, suffering for lack of them. As regards some of them at least, the comment in a recent American book is acute: that they are 'warnings of what will probably be the result of a certain kind of conduct rather than positive guides to action'. Further, they are 'excellent pedagogical devices for aiding the student of history, rather than rules of thumb for the direction of operations'.[1] However, the practice of compiling them is popular even with soldiers who have never written on any other subject. One famous military instructor, Marshal Foch, has given to two substantial volume of lectures the titles *Des Principles de la Guerre* and *De la Conduite de la Guerre*.

In a book published during the Second World War the present writer suggested that they might equally well be called ideals in warfare. He drew up a list of five.[2] It is proof of the fact that war is not an exact science when we find that the number framed by the experts varies and that the principles themselves often differ. Jomini and Foch both enumerated four, but on

---

[1] Preston, Wise, and Werner, *Men in Arms*, p. 3.
[2] Falls, *Ordeal by Battle*, p. 20.

their face they bear little resemblance to each other, though examination will show that they at least overlap. The author's five were the following: concentration, or economy of force: protection; surprise; aggressive reconnaissance, or readiness to fight for information; and maintenance of the aim.[3]

In wars between foes of equal military qualities—what the Germans call *ebenbürtig*—and anything approaching equal strength battles on land are seldom won without the concentration of superior strength at the vital point. It is as a principle simple and indeed obvious, but often far from simple in the execution. It generally involves risks elsewhere because it entails leaving inferior forces to face the enemy in other parts of the theatre of war or other sections of the front. The enemy may also be in a position to attack and may direct his blow against one of these weak places; he may even get it in first. The commander-in-chief is likely to be pestered by appeal from subordinates responsible for the defence of the weak places. If he is a strong-minded man he will disregard them, though some generals of justifiably high reputation have given way to them. In any case the subordinates will sometimes prove right.

One danger which may seem serious commonly ends as soon as a successful blow is struck. In theory,

---

[3] The actual title then given to the fifth was 'the undeviating thrust', devised because the writer desired to avoid the absurd English phrase, 'maintenance of the objective'. You cannot maintain an objective, but you can maintain the effort to reach it, that is, the aim. He has now decided to say so in the simplest words.

supposing the opposing forces to be equal, the weak places are still open to a counterstroke in similar superiority. In practice the initiative is a priceless asset and to wring it from the hands of the foe in possession of it is very difficult. The enemy may well have to divert a large proportion of the troops necessary for a counterstroke to patching up the part of the front which has been broken. The writer can recall how, as a military correspondent in the Second World War, after an offensive had been launched successfully he used to stare at the map and ask himself what the assailed army could do next. Most often the answer was in fact—nothing, except go on resisting or break contact with the attacker and regroup. The opportunities on the map were mirages. 'A beaten army is no longer in the hands of its general', wrote the Archduke Charles. This seeming platitude embodies a truth not always recognized. The implication is that the general cannot do with his beaten army what armchair critics consider he ought to do.

Protection has two functions. It is first of all an insurance policy against a surprise attack. Secondly, when an army is on the move, advanced and flank guards will often save the main body from deploying and thus undergoing needless fatigue. In a broader sense, the commander must never drop his guard.

Surprise is the most effective of all keys to victory. Successfully applied, this principle often brings results exceeding the brightest hopes of the commander who achieves it. It must always be considered in relation to the first principle, concentration, because the mingling of the element of surprise with concentration adds so greatly to the effect of the latter. Surprise in war seldom means quite the same thing as in other surroundings. It does not mean that the first intimation of trouble comes to the defence when it sees tanks and men charging forward because such a form of surprise is practically unattainable. It does not mean that the defence should have no inkling of what is about to happen. Usually the most to be hoped for—and it is a lot—is that the enemy should be caught so that he cannot alter his dispositions as he would have had there been no element of surprise. There are three types of surprise: the place, the time, and the weight. All three can rarely be attained, but two often have been. The chances can be increased by the use of ruses. The simplest kind is the pretence of doing something different from what the attacker means to do, sham preparation for attack elsewhere, for example, or leading the enemy to believe that the attacker's dispositions are other than they really are. Allenby's dummy horse-lines in Palestine, which misled the Turks about the position of his cavalry, is an example of this. A subtler and much rarer ruse, rare because so risky, is to make the real thing look like a feint clumsily prepared.

Aggressive reconnaissance is the present writer's own contribution—call it the bee in his bonnet. Reconnaissance should not entail fighting for fighting's sake; if the information needed can be got by stealth and guile, all the better. If, however, the choice is between fighting for information and fighting in the dark, the commander should not hestitate to opt for the former. Foch, though he did not include aggressive reconnaissance among the principles of war, insisted on its importance and his treatment of it is one of his chief contributions to military thought. He took from Napoleon the idea of a strong fighting advanced guard, led by an aggressive but well-balanced commander such as Lannes, always ready for a tussle to make the enemy disclose his intentions and confident of support from the main body when it runs into trouble, as it often will. The forcible ripping open of the enemy's screen may be the only means of discovering what lies behind it.

Lastly, maintenance of the aim enjoins the pursuance of the object until attained. The commander ought not to allow himself to be diverted from his aim by secondary objectives; nor should he fail to persevere in his attempt to reach it because his task proves more difficult than he had expected. Important though this principle is, however, it is subject to qualifications. Perseverance may develop into obstinacy, and from that to infatuation and wanton waste of life. On the other hand, a profitable opportunity may occur to change the aim in the midst of a battle; it may even be brought about by the reaction of the enemy to the effort to attain the aim and by the movements of his forces to block this effort. A classic example is to be found in the Battle of Alamein. Montgomery did not change his object, which was the destruction of the enemy's forces, but he did change his physical aim, the means to the end, in the course of the battle.

Next a few words must be devoted to characteristics of warfare. Here our friend Clausewitz is at his best, even though he does harp on the same string like a modern director of publicity. He was the first to examine thoroughly the moral element in war, the first to discuss with enlightenment the element of gambling, the first to say anything profitable about the element of friction, and, apparently, the inventor of the theory called the diminishing force of the offensive.

The moral element has two branches, the first of which may to a great extent govern the second: the qualities of the leadership and the spirit of the troops. Many pictures of the 'complete general' have been drawn, some of them making him such a paragon of all the virtues that they might be intended to depict a saint rather than a soldier, whereas on the whole saintliness is not a characteristic of the great commanders of history. 'Personal courage . . . boldness, resolution, imagination, patience, imperturbability, and resource-fulness' are the moral and mental virtues most needed in the commander-in-chief.[4] Personality is valuable but not essential. Soldiers are most inspired by obvious signs of competence and by success: personality falls flat if it does not produce anything but more crosses in the cemeteries and more occupied beds in the hospitals. Speeches to the troops belong to a very ancient tradition which has been carried into the most recent times. Yet opinion is not unanimous in their favour. Against Field-Marshal Lord Montgomery's

[4] Falls, *The Nature of Modern Warfare*, p. 85.

belief in them and success in delivering them must be set this remarkable comment of General de Gaulle: 'Condé at Rocroi, young though he was, bubbling with enthusiasm and surrounded by men eager to drink in his every word, mounted his horse, recon- noitred the battlefield, and rode down the lines with- out opening his lips, with the result that the troops immediately recognized in him a born soldier as well as a Prince of the Blood.'[5]

How much finer this sounds than the 'pep talk' or 'moral indoctrination' of today's jargon! Yet words assuredly count sometimes.

Patriotism and belief in the cause are obvious factors in the spirit of troops. The cynic will retort that belief in the cause is founded on passion or propaganda. It is often so, yet when the cause is bad or doubtful some men at least are assailed by qualms. Experience and training produce confidence. Experience—provided that it is not acquired too easily or in the wrong kind of war—is better than training; yet training may yield all the virtues of experience, as it did in the German Army of 1914. Gratitude shown by citation of units as well as by the decoration of individuals is a tonic.

Next, the element of gambling. Clausewitz declared that war resembled games in which competitors staked their money. Like poker, it is a game of chance as well as of skill and bluff. War is generally in some degree a gamble, and he who seeks certainties only is likely to miss every opportunity. Two opposite situations may lead a commander to gamble more boldly than he otherwise

[5] De Gaulle, *The Edge of the Sword*, p. 57.

would. They are the extremes of fortune: either he is so strong and his prospects are so good that failure to bring off a brilliant *coup* will not greatly prejudice him, and the venture is worth while, for instance, to end a war which may otherwise drag on too long; or it is a case of all or nothing because the situation is so bad that a limited victory is not worth while and nothing short of a miraculous triumph can be.

Metaphorical friction, says Clausewitz, is more potent in war than literal friction in mechanics. Those who have taken part in battles, perhaps most of all commanders and staff officers at the lower levels, can have no doubt about the truth of this assertion. They have groaned and shuddered while contemplating the effects of friction and striving to remedy them in time. The plan has been good and is developing well—then suddenly a maddening accident or misunderstanding occurs. Its direct and local influence is bad enough but the evil also spreads far and wide. Moreover, accidents do not always come singly. A chain of them is not an impossibility or an unknown calamity. Sometimes no human agency is at fault. Of all the causes of friction in war the weather is one of the most powerful. And, even in a great battle, the collapse of a single bridge beneath the weight of a tank may have deadly consequences.

The diminishing force of the offensive is one of the most obvious features of war, but the obvious is often enough overlooked. After a variable period of exertion, all forms of dynamic activity wholly or largely dependent

on human energy tend to decrease in effect proportionately to the energy employed. Let us not concern ourselves overmuch with the factor of fatigue
because it prevents the maintenance of the energy
imparted to the campaign at a constant strength.
Suppose that the commander on the offensive can use
fresh or rested troops to take the place of those growing
tired. Even then there will be a tendency for the force
of the offensive to diminish at a certain stage. The
machine will tire even if fresh troops are available.
As the distance covered grows supply will become
more and more difficult. Perhaps the strength of the
defence will increase, and its supply problems may
become easier while those of the attackers are becoming insoluble. The latter's vehicles may wear out—
and the more efficient self-propelled vehicles become,
the more complex are mobile workshops. The demo-
litions of the retreating army may prove a heavy brake.

The clearest proof that the conception of the diminishing force of the offensive is valid will be found in
the fact that the most successful offensives commonly
proceed in a series of bounds and the intervals between
them are used for reorganization and 'oiling the
machine'. But we must be clear that this is a factor
in a problem, not the problem itself. When we talk of
the diminishing force of the offensive we need not
imply that it will fall short of full success, to whatever
extent it may have to be prolonged. We merely point
to a weakness inherent in the offensive. Long before
that weakness becomes dangerous the enemy may be
down and out.

The last characteristic has been called 'the fog of war'. When we read the account of a battle or campaign compiled by a competent historian everything is clear to us. He may warn us that it is by no means always clear to the opposing commanders, who may make mistakes about the position or action of some part of their own forces, let alone those of the enemy. Such warnings do not always remain in the reader's consciousness, and when they do not the effect may be failure to realize why things happened, even though what did happen is not in doubt. Sometimes, as is common with fogs, the fog of war may lift or thin at some period of the battle or at some point on the battlefield and so permit at least a partial reconstruction of the enemy's dispositions and intentions. Sometimes there may be no fog. Again, uncertainty about what is going on 'on the other side of the hill' is a factor in warfare, not an element always present, but an important one.

What is all this theory worth? A general who gained distinction in the Second World War, Sir Brian Horrocks, remarked to the writer that he had never been able to understand any military theory. This was a polite way of saying that he thought it worthless and wondered why anybody took the trouble to compose or discuss it. No sane theorist nowadays offers solutions to the problems that arise on the battlefield. He may, as has already been suggested, provide warnings of what will be the probable results of certain actions. Surely nothing written in this introduction has been difficult to understand. Military theory is or should be a common-sense study of military cause and effect. It is a method by which we try to clear our minds as they become overcrowded by the events they have taken in. Anyhow, if there is an art of war, it is impossible to study it without theorizing. Every art has its theories.

This study begins with Napoleon. A single little volume covering warfare from the earliest known times would have been sketchy. The Napoleonic era, however, is not taken as a starting-point simply because one must start somewhere this side of the warfare of antiquity. It is suitable. When Marshal Foch began to work on his celebrated lectures delivered at the School of War he decided that wars before Napoleon's were of secondary interest to officers likely to be called upon to serve in a war of nations. He therefore confined his material to the wars of Napoleon and Moltke. Napoleon in war stands for the beginning of 'modern times'. A German contemporary of Napoleon not only came to this conclusion but founded his teaching and his fame upon it. Clausewitz saw war becoming, instead of a struggle between soverign and sovereign, a struggle between nation and nation.

In this warfare of peoples fighting for themselves instead of for more or less popular rulers, *fighting their own war*, numbers would increase and stakes would grow heavier. Wars for the sake of a province and 'wars of observation' would become rare; wars of decision and annihilation common. He pointed out that even before Napoleon had made himself master of

France, even before he had reached high command, the forces of the Revolution had inflicted defeat on those of the old-fashioned sovereignties: the Empire, Prussia, Spain, and Britain. He added that it was not until three Governments at least, those of Russia, the Empire, and Prussia took steps to broaden the basis of the war and make it correspond more closely to a people's war, that Napoleon's overthrow became certain. They did not, he remarked, go about the process thoroughly, but their greatly superior numbers made up for that deficiency.

'The more sublime and the stronger are the motives of a war', Clausewitz wrote, 'the more it embraces the total existence of peoples, the greater the tension that precedes a war, the closer will war approximate to its essential abstract power; the more its purpose will be to overthrow the enemy; the more strictly warlike, the less political, will be the spectacle of war.'

This was a remarkable comment, which has since influenced many thinkers and leaders, including Bismarck, Marx, and Hitler. What made it still more remarkable was the fact that Clausewitz when he wrote this passage could not have foreseen what was not made completely clear until the First World War, a century later, when for the purpose of waging war it was found necessary to mobilize and control virtually the whole nation. Nearly every form of activity was made subject to the demands of war. This process was carried a long step further in the Second World War, with one result even more catastrophic than any prophesied by Clausewitz. If the war was waged by nation against nation, then nation must attack nation; if the factory worker was as much a foe and was playing as big a part in the struggle as the sailor, the soldier, and the airman who used his products, then he too must be attacked. The new power of the bomber aircraft made this possible; indeed, the extreme inaccuracy of its aim prevented it from doing anything else. Now, however, the women too were flocking into the factories, even those most directly concerned with the tools of war. So the women also became the object of attack. The process did not stop even here. 'Industrial areas' became the admitted targets. So the housewives, the children, the infants in arms were included. Another stage was begun by the two atomic bombs dropped on Japan. All life in given areas had become the potential object of attack.

Napoleonic warfare had not led us to this point. It had nothing to do with flight or atomic energy; but it pointed the way to total war. There is thus ample justification for taking it as a starting-point.

This implies no belittlement of the precursors of Napoleon, though to find his equal one would have had to go back to Hannibal, if not to Alexander the Great. We are not called upon to decide that the army of Napoleon at Austerlitz was better or of greater interest than the army of Condé at Rocroi. Napoleon campaigned and fought on new principles, but like other innovators he made use of new conditions which he himself had not brought about, as Alva had first made use of mobile musketeers. So, great as may be our admiration for Napoleon as commander, it is for convenience that we begin with him. In one respect, however, we have to go a short way behind him. It would be clumsy and abrupt to begin with him without a preliminary glance back at the men who influenced him most directly.

Chapter One

PRE-NAPOLEONIC AND NAPOLEONIC
THEORY AND PRACTICE

THE French Army of Louis XVI was an improvement on that of the Seven Years War, from which France had emerged with, on the whole, a sorry record. Her infantry was still not the equal of the Prussian, but defeated armies often put more brains into study of the art of war and its development than those which have been victorious, and this was now the case. The French set themselves to learn from past errors, whereas the Prussians rested on their laurels and went on doing so until the disaster of Jena in 1806. The one advantage they retained was the ability of the infantry to fire faster than any in Europe, and even this, some French observers thought, was gained at the expense of failure to ram home the charge in the barrel.[1] The French artillery had been lightened and made more mobile without any serious loss of accuracy or range.

The Revolution broke up both Army and Navy, but whereas the former recovered fairly quickly, the sea service, which had reached its zenith under Louis XVI, never again attained that standard. The Army's recovery, however, was made possible only by the lethargy of the powers which went to war with France in the cause of what is named, according to the writer's political creed, legality or reaction. Prussia, Austria, Spain, and Britain were baffled by the tactics and

[1] Guibert, *Essay on Tactics*, Vol. i, p. 162.

daring of the revolutionary armies, even though these were raw in the extreme and sometimes given to shameful panic. On many occasions their lack of training produced an unorthodoxy which bewildered and shook their foes. They used skirmishers in greater force and actually with greater skill than had yet been witnessed in this century of the skirmisher, and their ragged advance and failure to keep alignment often presented to the view of the enemy one great swarm of skirmishers. It is an amazing spectacle, this of France facing successfully the professional armies of all western Europe upon her frontiers. She raised large armies by calling up volunteers in 1791 and by the great levies of 1793, followed by the highly successful amalgamation of the infantry of the line and the volunteers, one regular battalion to two volunteer in each demi-brigade. Remember that the regular rank and file remained and that without it volunteers and conscripts would have been useless.

Bonaparte's early days as an officer were passed in the turmoil of revolution, an atmosphere which he found invigorating. Even before it began, however, his talent and good luck led to contacts with the professional ability, the intellectual power, and the enthusiasm of French officers at their best. In the summer of 1788 he served with his regiment at the Artillery School of Auxonne. The commandant, the Baron du Theil, was an able gunner, who encouraged the twenty-year-old officer to study not only the arm in which he proposed to make his career but the whole art of war. He knew well the commandant's younger brother, the Chevalier du Theil, and read his remarkable little work on the tactics of the new artillery which has been mentioned. He certainly read—for every intelligent French officer was reading it and there was already an English translation[2]—a more famous work, the *Essai générale de Tactique* of Hippolyte de Guibert. Guibert was more than a brilliant student of tactics. He was a man of genius, a seer who gazed into the future and discovered its most profound and far-reaching secret. Having analysed the military weaknesses of the powers of his time, he exclaimed: 'But suppose there were to spring up in Europe a vigorous people, possessed of genius, power, and a favourable form of government; a people who combined with the virtues of austerity and a national soldiery a fixed plan of aggrandizement; who never lost sight of this system; who, knowing how to wage war at small cost and subsist by its victories, could not be reduced by financial considerations to laying down its arms. We should see this people subjugate its neighbours and overthrow our feeble constitutions, as the north wind bends the slender reeds.'[3]

Here is pure inspiration. The conception is that of a nation in arms, such as France was to become. Though it is expressed with complete disregard of humanity, he was far from insensitive to such ideals. He was a prophet and a philosopher. What Clausewitz and Jomini discussed after the event, the terrific outburst of energy which follows on the heels of a revolution

[2] Published in 1781. A copy lies on the table on which these lines are written.

[3] Guibert, *Essai générale de Tactique*, Vol. i, p. xiii.

that is not merely political but also intellectual and spiritual, a revolution in men's minds and hearts as well as in their laws and behaviour, Guibert had foreseen. He died in 1790 before his vision came true.

Speed and elasticity were the ideals of Guibert: officers and rank and file must be trained to manœuvre fast. For advanced training he prescribed camps of a division at least and up to three infantry and two cavalry divisions, 40,000 men. They should practise tasks such as forced marches, the passage of rivers, and especially forming column from line for advance or manœuvre and deploying from column to line for fighting. Generals must learn not to deploy—that is, form into order of battle—until close to and within sight of the enemy. The effects of premature deployment had been time and time again that the dispositions or frontage were unsuitable when battle was joined, either because strength had been concentrated at the wrong place or because the enemy had revised his dispositions. The armies of Guibert's day were unable to delay their deployment as he proposed because they could not take the risk in view of their slow methods. He showed how the change from column to line and *vice versa* could be simplified and speeded up, so that either line or column could be formed quickly to right, to left, or—the greatest novelty—on the centre.

The infantry should fight three deep, as that of Frederick the Great had fought against armies which adopted a depth of as much as six ranks. This Guibert would never countenance, except in a completely open plain in which infantry might have to face both ways

Diagram I

PRE-NAPOLEONIC: THREE OF GUIBERT'S INFANTRY EVOLUTIONS

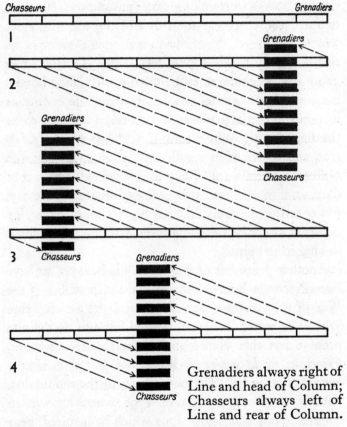

Grenadiers always right of Line and head of Column; Chasseurs always left of Line and rear of Column.

1. Battalion in Line. 2. Forming Column on right from Line. 3. Forming Column on left from Line. 4. Forming Column on centre from Line.

if cavalry attacked it in rear. His bugbear was clumsiness. He denounced the doctrine of assault in column and declared it to be pure illusion that depth gave weight to the attack. Even for cavalry he preferred, as a general attack formation, two ranks only. He condemned the charge at the trot and the use of pistols, which, he urged, generally meant that there was no real charge but only a pointless scuffle. On the other hand, it was useless to end a charge with jaded horses. Suppose that it started 600 paces from the enemy or just beyond effective musketry fire, it should cover the first 200 paces at a slow trot, the second at a fast trot, and the third at a gallop. Though cavalry was to Guibert's mind a valuable arm, he ranked it as secondary, an arm of opportunity, for exploitation of victory, for covering an army in retreat. It should never, he declared, attack infantry unless the latter were disordered or shaken in spirit.

Another preceptor of Napoleon's is believed to have been Pierre de Bourcet, the brilliant staff officer of the War of the Austrian Succession and the Seven Years War. The world 'believed' is used because no definite proof exists that Napoleon had read Bourcet's work, *Principles de la guerre de montagnes*, but it is almost certain that he had. His own tactics in the mountains, notably in the campaign of 1796 when he was in command but also that of 1794 which he inspired, bear the marks of Bourcet's ideas, though the genius which exploited them was his own. In one instance his dispositions almost reproduce Bourcet's, but this might be because, fighting on the same ground, he knew from

another source how it had been used. Bourcet points
out that in mountain warfare the roads are more important than in any other type because no such movement across country as can commonly be carried out
in the plains is possible. At the same time roads through
mountains are almost always fewer than in plains.
Therefore every practicable route should be used.
This may involve separating columns more widely
than in normal country, but there is little danger in
moving troops through mountains in 'little packets'
such as it would be lunacy to employ in the former,
equally close to the enemy. In the mountains they are
not only relatively safe but necessary because otherwise there would be no possibility of forcing a way
through. The attacker must mystify the defence by
feints. He must be prepared to turn a feint into the
real thing. Every plan must, says Bourcet, have 'a
second and a third branch'. This will enable the attacker
to turn hostile positions or by manœuvre induce the
defence to uncover or weaken them. Flexibility and
bluff provide the best means of avoiding frontal attacks
against strong mountain positions, attacks which may
often fail and in any case will commonly prove costly.
At the same time every marching column must be
covered by detachments on ground commanding its
road so that fire may not be brought to bear upon it.
All this is peculiar to mountain warfare. Bourcet's
doctrine of elasticity has, however, a wider application.
It is exemplified by the columns resembling the
suckered arms of an octopus in the campaigns of Ulm
and Austerlitz.

It is natural that the French writers, Pierron and Colin, who traced the connexion between Napoleon's miltary education and his tactics, and the English writers, Spenser Wilkinson and Liddell Hart, who later discussed them, should somewhat over-estimate his debt to his instructors and to the remarkable pre-revolutionary literature of his profession. Napoleon was a commander of the highest genius, who stands with Alexander and Hannibal, making up the greatest trio of captains in the annals of war. Such men transform war; they do not conform to the precepts of writers. Yet even the greatest soldiers are influenced in their ideas and background by what they have been taught and what they have read, and Napoleon was not only an enthusiastic reader but a firm believer in the value of the study of military history. When taking over command in Italy in 1796 he sent for a history of the campaigns of Maillebois in the mountains in which he himself was to fight. Of all hands, this fell into those of Nelson, who found the parcel of books in a captured ship. 'The Directory, it would appear, wish to instruct him; pray God he may remain ignorant', wrote Nelson. However, the General-in-Chief of the Army of Italy obtained another copy.[4]

Thus, Napoleon inherited not only an enterprising and dashing army, with a fine record against foes of superior strength, but a profusion of conceptions and precepts which fortified his genius. The combination

[4] Wilkinson, *The Rise of General Bonaparte*, p. 80. The book in question is *Histoire des campagnes de M. le Maréchal de Maillebois en Italia* . . . par M. le Marquis de Pézay. Bourcet was staff officer to Maillebois.

of such a leader and such an army produced tremendous power. Not that it was full-fledged in 1796 or even when he became First Consul at the end of 1799. He transformed it in the following years. The infantry was the best arm, but he had to improve its discipline. Little was wrong with the artillery except that there was not nearly enough of it and that too much of what was available was tied to the infantry. He expanded it greatly and set it free. He turned the hired drivers into soldiers. The cavalry, as the most expensive arm, was, naturally in a bankrupt country, the weakest numerically in relation to its tasks, and its movements were virtually confined to the battlefield and the line of march in company with the other two arms. The cavalry Napoleon also expanded and released from its fetters. Unlike that of Frederick the Great, magnificent on the field of battle but narrow in its range, Napoleon's cavalry moved wide and deep on reconnaissance and pursued a beaten enemy with fury.[5]

Napoleon's strategy was not uniform throughout his active career. The First and Second Italian campaigns and the campaign in Egypt were conducted with forces small by comparison with the Grand Army of the Empire. In the First Italian campaign some 35,000 men were commonly spread over a front of 20 miles or more and victories were won by manœuvring so as to bring superior strength to bear successively on sections of the enemy's still more extended front. The object was to separate the Austrian and Piedmontese armies,

[5] Becke, Captain A. F., *Introduction to the History of Tactics*, pp. 9, 23, 29.

then drive the latter out of the war, and finally deal with the Austrians alone. From 1806, the year of Jena, Napoleon developed a new technique more suitable to an army 200,000 strong, rather less well trained in consequence of its expansion, and as time went on including a growing proportion of troops other than French. He had already introduced the army corps, consisting of two or three divisions with cavalry attached when necessary. Now he used a strong army corps as advanced guard. Its function was to engage the enemy when met and pin him to his ground, so that the remaining corps could manœuvre with precision to deal the shattering blow which became the feature of Napoleonic battles. These corps advanced in a lozenge formation, so that one on either wing was quickly available to come upon the flank of the advanced guard. The rearmost piece was the general reserve, the Imperial Guard, held jealously under the Emperor's own hand. For the battle he would mass artillery— the maximum was 200 guns at Borodino—to carry out his preparation for the assault. He saw with his own eyes when the time was ripe and the enemy's powers were waning. 'Then at his signal the massed batteries of the Guard reserve dashed to the front at a gallop, unlimbered within 500 yards of the enemy, and proceeded to tear with extreme rapidity a hole with case-shot in the opposing battle formation.[6]

It is certainly a less arresting and artistic picture than that of the First Italian campaign. Some commentators have condemned it as reactionary and

[6] Becke, *Introduction to the History of Tactics*, p. 31.

alleged that it marked a degeneration of the Emperor's genius. Liddell Hart puts it that 'General Bonaparte' applied a theory which brought him his empire and 'the Emperor Napoleon' developed a practice which wrecked it.[7] We must recall, however, that the First Italian campaign was genuine mountain warfare and that Napoleon was never again called upon to wage this kind of war exclusively. And we must not forget that he had to face the full might of his foes from 1806, whereas in 1796 the Italian theatre was for the Austrians a secondary matter and while they were suffering defeat there the Archduke Charles with their main army was whipping the French in Germany. Finally, there was little sign of degeneracy in 1814 when Napoleon found himself facing enormous odds in his defence of France against Austrian, Prussian, and Russian forces. Then he returned to the earlier form of manœuvre, and none of his achievements in Italy eighteen years before was more dazzling.

Napoleon appreciated the virtues of the men he led, but he understood their failings also. The former were invaluable. The French private soldier was the most intelligent in Europe. He took more interest in winning a battle and in its tactics, the Emperor affirmed, than a Russian officer. He possessed bravery 'of an impatient sort' and a sense of honour that fitted him for great deeds. He was the only soldier in Europe who would go on fighting on an empty stomach. He was tireless in pursuit of a beaten foe. These qualities made the seasoned troops of the Army of Italy a

[7] Hart, *The Ghost of Napoleon*, p. 102.

marvellous weapon in the hands of a commander such as the young Bonaparte. And though, as stated, some deterioration followed, his power after every campaign up to the invasion of Russia to recover all prisoners of war except those taken by the British—and all taken up to the Treaty of Amiens even by them—provided him with experienced men to leaven the drafts.

The worst faults of French troops were unruliness and resentment of discipline, though this was milder than in any contemporary army, and a tendency to extreme discouragement after defeat. By contrast, in Napoleon's view, defeat weakened the spirit of the German and Russian soldier hardly at all.[8] This was the natural obverse of the French soldier's virtues. The French Army under Napoleon was eager, active, frugal, and enduring, but in spirit rather fragile in the hands of some of his commanders. In his it remained stout and loyal to the end. In 1814 even the untrained lads whom he was forced to call to the colours fought gallantly against the best Austrian and Prussian units.

The most formidable army which the French had to face in the last years of the eighteenth century and the first few years of the nineteenth was that of Austria, still, until 1806, ruled by the Holy Roman Emperor. Moreover, in the campaigns which brought Napoleon down and forced him to abdicate in 1814, Austria contributed the largest contingent. Then, as always, the troops were drawn from a medley of races speaking different languages and uneven in quality. The general level was, however, good. The cavalry was accounted

[8] Herold, *The Mind of Napoleon*, p. 215.

the best in Europe. Staff work was reliable, if slow. The Russian commander Suvarov employed Austrian staff officers in Italy, though this in itself is not a high tribute to their skill because the Russian standard was so low.

We are apt to underrate the old or elderly commanders who opposed Napoleon in Italy in 1796 and 1800. They were in fact competent and energetic. Their misfortune was that Napoleon was about a generation ahead of them in tactics. The only important success gained by the French before he took command was that won by Schérer in 1794, and then both strategy and tactics had been laid down by General Bonaparte. Austrian troops with the highest class leadership were very good indeed, and Austria did produce one great soldier in these wars.

Wellington thought the Archduke Charles the outstanding commander on the allied side but kept from reaching his full height by bad health. He was subject to trances which suggested epilepsy. Born in 1771, two years later than Napoleon and Wellington, his campaign of 1796 in Germany, in which he drove the French armies of Moreau and Jourdan over the Rhine, has been quoted and analysed almost as much as Napoleon's in Italy in the same year. He was a student of tactics and an excellent historian. He was personally gallant and determined; at Aspern he was so well up in front, urging his troops forward, that the French could recognize him without telescopes. And Aspern was the first defeat in the open field inflicted on Napoleon.

Yet, though he was the Emperor's brother, the Archduke seldom appeared to get the last ounce out of his army, as Napoleon, Wellington, and even Masséna could out of theirs. Aspern was certainly an important French defeat, but it was nearly a disaster and ought to have been one. Failure to clinch the success led to Napoleon's recovery and his hard-won victory of Wagram. Dissatisfaction with his brother's conduct of both battles and a personal jealousy, discreditable but not untypical of the House of Habsburg, induced the Emperor to make a change in the supreme command. Under Prince Schwarzenberg the Austrian troops fought well, but there was no flame in them any more than in their leader. They were good, willing soldiers; but, even if the Archduke had possessed a higher appeal, even if Schwarzenberg had possessed his military skill, the lower leadership was not quite alert enough.

The Russian Army, that which pushed Napoleon on to the downward path to utter defeat, was slow-footed and primitive in its methods. The British officers who fought beside the Russian contingent in Holland were as much astonished by its clumsiness as East Anglians were by its habits when they saw Russian soldiers drinking the oil out of their street lamps. It was, however, always sound in defence and nearly always prepared to attack, however badly led. One of its commanders should be popular with those who hold that character is far more important than brains. Suvarov was by no means well endowed with brains, but he had the spirit of half a dozen leaders of average worth. We talk too often of soldiers worshipping their commanders, which is indeed, even in the conventional use of the word, a rare state of affairs; but in that sense it is true of the relations between Suvarov and his men. And so in Italy, while Bonaparte was conveniently exiled in Egypt and the Russian and Austrian allies enjoyed superior strength, Suvarov crushed the French and wrenched from them virtually all their gains. Little or no finesse entered into his methods. He used his infantry as a battering ram and it was pleased and proud to play the part.

Despite its achievement in Italy, however, the Russian Army was seen at its best in the immemorial role of defending its own soil in 1812. In modern terms it was 'defence in depth' carried to the extreme limit. The immensity of the country supplied the place of Russian generalship, which was commonplace. The ferocious cold of the Russian winter proved a faithful and powerful ally, not for the first time and by no means for the last. The campaign was won by strategy rather than tactics, and it is of interest to note that it was a general of foreign blood, Barclay de Tolly, who led Napoleon into the depths of Russia and was discarded as over-timid when he had prepared the way for the French disaster. He was succeeded by Kutusov, a fighter occasionally, but far from a genius.

Mention has been made of Prussian complacency and stagnation after the death of Frederick the Great. In 1806 Prussia, having missed a great chance to come in in 1805, the year of Austerlitz, challenged Napoleon at an unfavourable moment, without awaiting aid from Russia and when he was prepared: he was superintending the setting up of the Confederation of the

Rhine and the bulk of the Grand Army was in Germany. The Prussian Army was by now 'a museum specimen, organized and ordered to fight ranged battles on level ground—phalanx against phalanx—in which a volley fired by a carefully dressed line of men at 40 to 50 paces from the enemy was the decisive factor'.[9] Had it been allowed to pick a suitable plain, form up at its leisure, and meet a purely frontal attack, it could have blasted the French or any other foe to perdition, but it got no such opportunity. Instead it was overwhelmed by case-shot and the devastating fire of French skirmishers and finally broken by a general advance. The campaign is notable for one of the fiercest and most relentless pursuits in military history, in which Murat and his cavalry distinguished themselves particularly. This pursuit was more deadly than the French fire on the battlefield. Section after section of the beaten army surrendered shamefully at the first summons. Prussia was left helpless. Napoleon well understood the value of pursuit, but even he never brought off another of this sort.

Only after the French disaster in Russia could Prussia raise her head again. Then, owing to the way in which Scharnhorst had nursed the little flame in the remnant of an army permitted by Napoleon and to the daring and courage of the new leader, Blücher, the performance was a fine one. Of the armies under the supreme command of Schwarzenberg which fought Napoleon in Germany and France, the Prussian was the most enterprising. Its tactics were still less effective

[9] Fuller, *The Decisive Battles*, Vol. ii, p. 418.

than the French. The great change was in heart, and this was exemplified not only in the final campaign of France in 1814, but after Napoleon's return from exile and the resumption of war, at Ligny and Waterloo.

The British Army varied in quality. It was at its best when it had been seasoned under Wellington's leadership in the Peninsula, but it had previously fought admirably under Abercromby in Egypt, where it established such an ascendancy over the French that it finally cowed rather than forced them into surrender. Sir John Moore's famous training camp at Shorncliffe not only provided excellent skirmishing troops, armed with an early rifle, but exercised an influence in favour of speed and skill in manœuvre. Yet the Army was fated by circumstances to fight most commonly on the defensive. Despite Salamanca and some other fine displays in attack, the French regarded the British infantryman as essentially a defensive fighter, and the most thoughtful observers—and sufferers at his hands—such as Foy and the young Bugeaud, accounted him the best in the world in that role. The cavalry was well mounted and its shock was terrific. Most of its leadership was, however, so rash that Wellington, though he considered it capable of riding over a superior force of French cavalry, became nervous about launching it against an inferior one, lest it should be surprised and cut to pieces.

Wellington in the Peninsula had a liking for a method called strategic offensive with tactical defensive. The meaning of the phrase is that he would advance rapidly into the heart of the enemy's country but when

confronted by one of the French armies would stand
and fight a defensive battle. It is a good principle for
an army faced by heavy odds, provided it is reliable and
well commanded. The British Army sought the type
of position so characteristic that it has become known
as 'Wellingtonian'. The main body was drawn up in
two lines—a formation adopted in the Peninsula
despite the fact that the official regulation prescribed
three—behind the crest of a gentle slope. The French
advance up the slope was contested by the light troops,
and when these had been driven in was faced by the
main body, which as Bugeaud put it, 'silent and
impressive, with ported arms, loomed like a long red
wall.'[10] Finally came a crashing volley, and the battle
was as good as won.

Controversy has been aroused as to how it came
about that the French were so frequently caught in
columns, which meant that, apart from their skirmishers, only a small proportion of the attacking force
could use its muskets, whereas every man of Wellington's double line could fire deliberately. The older
school, including Fortescue and Oman, followed by
a majority of commentators, hold that the French
always intended to assault in columns and to bullock
through by a combination of bluff and weight, after
leaving the shooting to their skirmishers. The later
school, to which Colin was converted, says, broadly
speaking, that the troops remained in column too long,
largely because they had misjudged the moment for
deployment into line. Its leading exponents, Colin and

[10] Quimby, *The Background of Napoleonic Warfare*, p. 125.

Becke, go back to the orders issued to the French troops and show that in some cases these enjoined deployment. They also produce instances of French columns having tried to deploy but having left it too late. There can be little doubt that the new school is correct in its view that this is what generally happened; also that deployment for assault was in accordance with the French doctrine established by the beginning of the nineteenth century. Napoleon himself, when he came to command a large army divided into corps, often far apart and sometimes fighting their own battles, as in the Jena, Friedland, Eckmühl, and Waterloo campaigns, did not often dictate the formation for the attack. When he did, he prescribed neither the *ordre profound* (column) nor the *ordre mince* (line) but the *ordre mixte*. This was a formation of battalions in line and others in column, the role of the latter being to exploit success, form front in another direction, or undertake any other action called for. It has also been suggested that the French commanders did not deploy because they had often scared other opponents by the appearance of their columns. This would explain their early methods against Wellington, but later they lost confidence in themselves and felt pessimistic about the prospects of their attacks. The most that can be allowed is that on a few occasions a commander kept his troops in column because he feared that if they were shaken out and less fully under his control they would make off to the rear.[11]

[11] The two sides in this interesting dispute are represented by Becke—a brave pioneer of the 'new school' attacking the

The art of war developed in the Napoleonic era as Guibert had foreseen in his vision of 'a vigorous people, with genius, with power, and a happy form of government', that is to say, it tended to concern a war of peoples and to be animated by the ideas proper to such a state of affairs. As Clausewitz says, it was only in France that the concept of a people's war reached what he held to be its ideal form, but the Archduke Charles in Austria, Tsar Alexander in Russia, and above all Scharnhorst in Prussia were all touched by the concept. The rulers and Governments did not go as far along the path as the French because their countries had not been revolutionized, but they went far enough to be able to overcome him with superior numbers. In the context of this study insistence has naturally been laid on mobility, speed, and manœuvre, but other changes occurred. Fortresses still played a part and sieges were carried out, but the latter became rarer because with improved roads and diminished baggage trains fortresses did not block movement as before. Armies had been liberated. The darker side was the hardship inflicted on countries by armies subsisting on them, leading to savage guerrilla warfare, especially in Spain, and savage reprisals; to more frequent disregard of neutrality to shorten marches and aid manœuvre. In these and some other ways the new agility of armies pointed to the 'totality' of war and its unhappy consequences.

experts and the generally accepted evidence: Colin in *Les Transformations de la Guerre*; and Quimby. For the old school stand Oman in *Studies in the Napoleonic Wars*, and Fortescue in *A History of the British Army*.

Chapter Two

SEA WARFARE IN THE AGE
OF SAIL

THE main and ultimate object of combatant naval forces is to obtain command of the sea, omitting such waters as it is clearly impossible to enter or which are not required. The main purpose of such command is the security of sea routes and the denial of their use to an enemy in time of war. The best means of obtaining command is the defeat of the enemy in battle.

All these statements need some qualification, and lengthy volumes have been written in argument about how far they are valid. In the first place, absolute command of the sea is nineteen times out of twenty unobtainable; the almost invariable state of affairs in a naval war is a disputed command, with one side in the ascendant. Then, nations with no hope of achieving command of the sea provide themselves with small navies useful as convoy escorts, for coast defence, and for other tasks. When two opposing navies can put to sea at once the security of sea routes is never complete in the case of the stronger, and the denial may not be complete in that of the weaker. Sea routes are unlike the land routes of an army in that both sides and even the trade of both sides may occasionally use the same ones. Finally, defeat of the enemy in battle often has to be postponed. Before the days of submarines and air forces a belligerent could place its fleet in an unassailable anchorage and await its time. Sometimes the aim is virtually abandoned, as it was by Britain in the First World War, though her superiority of strength over Germany was very great.[1] Yet it is a mistake to suppose that the complete containment or unbreakable blockade of a hostile fleet can be as satisfactory as its destruction in battle. There is no full substitute for victory. A war may certainly be won even though the enemy remains undefeated at sea, but so long as he maintains 'a fleet in being' it will continue to be a dangerous factor. Even victory is not enough unless annihilating in nature. This conception was never absent from the mind of Nelson. On several occasions he is recorded as using the word 'annihiliation'. Half an hour before he died in his flagship at Trafalgar he demanded of Hardy how many ships had been captured and, on being told at least fourteen or fifteen, made the comment: 'I bargained for twenty.' The weakness of the best English naval historian and theorist, Sir Julian Corbett, is his belittlement of the doctrine of 'seeking out and destroying the enemy'.

A nation which lives largely by foreign trade and has incurred heavy responsibilities beyond the seas in encouraging and protecting it, as was already the case with Britain in the Napoleonic wars, puts its confidence in its navy above all. The fact that Great Britain and Ireland were islands and that a navy provided the best means of defence against invasion increased this dependence on the sea service. Possessing this unique

[1] Falls, *The First World War*, p. 342.

form of power, Britain was tempted to wage war by strangling at sea the trade of her continental foes, mainly the French since the decline of the power of Spain, subsidizing her allies, and keeping out of heavy commitments on land. Time after time, however, she was forced to modify this policy because in its naked form it would have led to the defeat of her allies or their refusal to continue the struggle beside a partner unwilling to dirty her boots.

Even then her wars were based on sea power. The Royal Navy permitted her to move troops where she desired and generally prevented the enemy from doing so by sea, though not always. If possible she sent them to vital theatres such as the Netherlands and Germany. If an overwhelmingly strong land power dominated the continent of Europe and struck down her allies, Britain could still transport her small armies to strategic points where they would not be overwhelmed by weight of numbers or where they would keep valuable bases out of the enemy's hands. Many operations of this kind were carried out in the Napoleonic Wars, including the seizure of Minorca, Corsica, and Malta and the occupation of Sicily, the expeditions to the West Indies and to Egypt, and the long campaigns in the Iberian Peninsula.

In one case Britain closely supported a friendly army which had its flank on the sea. This occasion marked the beginning of the conflict between two young warriors of genius. The younger, by eleven years, was twenty-six in 1795, but already the higher in rank. Bonaparte was not actually on the scene but was directing the campaign in Italy from Paris. Nelson commanded a small detached squadron, including only one ship of the line. Yet his grip on the Riviera was so tight that, according to Bonaparte, supply traffic was brought to an end. After the latter had defeated the Piedmontese in the spring of 1796 and separated them from the Austrians the situation was reversed. Nelson, like Bonaparte before him, acknowledged his discomfiture. The defence had been so strengthened, he wrote, that there were new 'batteries from one end of the coast to the other, within shot of each other' and it was virtually impossible to cut out a convoy. This was a strategic tussle between sea and land forces, but at very close quarters.

In studying sea warfare in the age of sail, a great ally to reading would be experience of yachting, not so much as regards navigation as weather and tides. Yet, while the experienced yachtsman cannot fail to find himself furnished with the means to understand the tactical problems of the old admirals, their much simpler strategic problems may not so readily occur to him. They may be simple, but they are often none the less difficult to solve.

For example, in that eventful year, 1796, Admiral Lord Bridport, with base at Spithead, was blockading a French fleet in Brest, and was aware that an expeditionary force was being prepared close to that port. It was largely owing to the looseness or slackness of the blockade that the French fleet and its transports got out, and the danger was the greater because the position of Brest made it virtually impossible for the main body of the Channel Fleet in the Solent to catch the enemy unless his destination was up Channel. To make matters worse, Bridport found himself 'embayed'—that is, he could not beat out into the open —for several days, and kicked his heels in an absurd state of helplessness while the French were doing as they liked. Luckily for Britain, the French fleet met with extremely hard weather and, after remaining for some time in Bantry Bay, abandoned the hope of landing troops and sailed for home. It got back, however, without sighting a ship of the Channel fleet. And there can be no doubt that if the army had succeeded in landing from its transports it would have speedily overrun all Ireland.

Reflecting on this episode and his own experience later on in the war, when he commanded the Channel Fleet, Lord St. Vincent concluded that Spithead would not do as a base, even though he was maintaining a ferocious close blockade, very different from Bridport's, of a far larger fleet, the main naval strength of France and Spain combined. If, he reasoned, the combined fleets did contrive to get out in the prevailing south-westerly wind, they would be so far to windward of the reserve of the Channel Fleet in the Solent—Brest being roughly 200 miles south-west of Portsmouth—that while the British were beating down Channel the French and Spaniards would gain a dangerous start for Ireland, for the West Indies, or for the Mediterranean. He therefore established a new base at Torbay, 115 miles W.S.W. of Portsmouth. So, in days of sail, the situation of a naval base in terms of prevailing winds was highly important. And if its exit pointed in the direction of the prevailing wind it was *ipso facto* a poor base in certain circumstances.

Again, when Nelson arrived from home to take command of the fleet blockading the Franco-Spanish fleet under Villeneuve in Cadiz in 1805, he found the main body cruising about twenty miles off the port and drew it back to about fifty. Those who guess the reason without previous knowledge of the subject will be entitled to claim perspicacity. Because a hard westerly wind might force his somewhat unwieldy three-deckers[2] into the Mediterranean, whither the fleet as a whole would then have to go too, and he might not be able to get out again for some time. He retained bitter memories of being caged by a head wind in the Straits of Gibraltar. Of course he kept an inshore squadron within sight of the enemy and in touch with the flagship by signal.

Pre-arranged signals played a big part in the efficiency of a fleet and were provided for many situations. Howe laid down that a blue pennant at the fore topmast-head was an order to break through the enemy's van, at the main to break through his centre, and at the mizzen to break through his rear. There were precise signals for making more sail or reducing it, and

---

[2] The standard ship of the line was the two-decker, normally mounting seventy-four guns. She was an all-purpose ship, the ship that won the naval war. The three-deckers were used to strengthen the line in battle and might number from one in four to one in eight of the battle fleet. At Trafalgar Nelson had seven, the Spaniards four, and the French one. Three-deckers were not good ships for close blockade.

captains were required to know what was needed in order to keep their rate constant with that of the admiral. Nelson had special signals ordering captains to engage the enemy's starboard or port side.[3]

A characteristic of naval strategy was the tendency of one side, the weaker either from the start or after defeat, to concentrate on commerce raiding. For this purpose it employed ships of its national navy, or more often privateers. After Trafalgar French privateers captured thousands of British vessels. The blows were distressing, but, as in former examples of the *guerre de course*, they were far from being mortal. The significance of this strategy was that the country which took to it abandoned completely the hope of using the sea for its trade, whereas its foe with a navy supreme at sea maintained its merchant fleet, even though this lost heavily.

The above are only jottings on naval strategy, but all there is room for here. We must go on to tactics.

British tactics were sometimes clumsy, but they were healthy, except from the enemy's point of view. Their object was nearly always to come to close quarters with him and strike at the hulls of his ships. In general everyone, from the admiral to the powder-monkey, went into action with confidence because they knew that British gunners could serve and fire their guns much more rapidly than the enemy. The business of the fleet was often concerned with land forces or with convoys, but even so the doctrine was

[3] Corbett, *Fighting Instructions, 1530-1816*, pp. 243–5, 271, 281.

that the enemy should if possible be put out of action, not merely held off. Nelson put it bluntly that the job of a commander-in-chief was, first to lay his ships 'close on board the enemy as expeditiously as possible, and, secondly, to continue them there without separating until the business is decided'. [4]

The French officers, on the other hand, looked on their fleets as the guardians and servants of their armies and convoys purely and simply, and, when engaged in that role considered that decisive action should be avoided provided hostile fleets could be kept out of the way by other means. They were thus accustomed to open fire at longer range than the British and aim higher, in the hope of disabling a ship by hitting a mast or spar. Of the other maritime peoples, the British had, as of old, found the Dutch as determined as themselves, but after Camperdown in 1797 they never had to meet a Dutch fleet. They were to find in 1812 that the ships of the United States were ready to 'swap punches'.

How was the British ideal of close action to prevail, whether or not the enemy wanted it? Ideas developed through a line of magnificent admirals: Rodney, Hood, Howe, St. Vincent to Nelson—who had himself served under all but Rodney. The order of battle had become more or less stereotyped as single line ahead, that is the equivalent of single file on land. Often enough two fleets engaged each other on opposite tacks and sailed past each other, every ship firing at successive targets as they passed, and the whole thing was speedily over

[4] Corbett, *Fighting Instructions, 1530–1816*, p. 313.

with trifling damage to either side. Even when they sailed parallel on the same tack it was not always easy to get to close quarters with an enemy who opened out the distance and re-formed his line. The solution which emerged was to break his line at one, two, or even more points and engage part of it on the other side.

Nelson's first master-stroke, which brought him fame, occurred under the command of Sir John Jervis, who took the title of Earl St.Vincent from the Spanish cape which gave the battle its name. It was a brilliant step to prevent the junction of two sections of the Spanish fleet.

The opposing fleets sighted one another on 14 February 1797. The Spaniards were making for Cadiz running E.S.E. before the wind in two sections, the foremost of six ships, the main body of twenty-one. The English, fifteen sail of the line, were sailing south in two columns. Jervis formed the fleet in single column, his object being to pass between the two Spanish divisions, go about, and attack the larger to windward. Three Spanish ships from the larger division managed to cross ahead of Jervis and join the smaller leeward division, raising it to nine. Perhaps Jervis left it slightly too long before tacking in succession and wheeling northward. At all events Nelson in the *Captain*, last but two ships in the line, saw the main enemy fleet turn north, evidently with the intention of passing behind Jervis and joining their leeward division. He also saw that the move was likely to succeed. Still a long way short of the turning point, he left the line, 'took a short cut', and engaged the first Spanish ship he could come up with. Troubridge in the

Culloden, the leading British ship, which had turned some time before and was sailing northward, at once on his own initiative steered to join him. Two other ships were signalled by Jervis to do likewise. The Spaniards were forced into a dog-fight. Nelson's boarding of the *San Nicolas* and, across her deck— 'Nelson's patent bridge', as the fleet called it later— of the *San Josef* is immortal, but it would have been impossible without this superb personal initiative.

This incident has been picked out of many tactical expedients because it illustrates Nelson's passion for getting to close quarters. Let us see how this was illustrated in his last and most decisive battle, Trafalgar.

The main principle on which he worked had long been in his mind and had already been exploited in the Battle of the Nile. It was to bring superior strength to bear against one part of the enemy's line and destroy that to start with; but his conception of how it was to be done was subject to flux. Before leaving England he told Lord Sidmouth that he would break the enemy's line in two places, with two lines led by himself and Collingwood. He kept to the notion of dividing his fleet into two columns, but next evolved a scheme whereby Collingwood should make the first attack on the allied rear, 'doubling' on—that is, placing ships on either side of—a number of the French and Spanish ships—while Nelson, with the other half of the fleet, awaited the opportunity to deal the decisive blow at the most effective point. Yet when battle was joined on 21 October, only ten days after the last plan had been made, the attack differed from that foreseen in both plans. 'As Ivanhoe, at the instant of encounter in the lists, shifted his lance from the shield to the casque of the Templar, Nelson, at the moment of engaging, changed the details of his plan, and substituted an attack in two columns, simultaneously made.'[5] These two columns, by then nearly two miles apart, struck the enemy's line at right angles, Collingwood's the further towards its rear, but still not far rearward of its centre.

In the light breeze of that day the movement was painfully slow and the leading ships had to endure heavy fire before they could bring their own broadsides into action. The consequence was that the four leading ships, two in each column, suffered one-third of all the British losses. But the heads of each column broke through the allied line at several points, engaged hostile ships on the far (leeward) side, and paved the way for the decisive and crushing victory won by the ships which followed. Eighteen hostile ships were taken or destroyed. The tactics which reduced the battle to a series of single-ship actions, at heavy odds to start with, depended on superior gunnery, which Nelson knew he possessed.

No other naval battle was fought in this war and when it came to an end in 1815 the earliest steam warship, especially built to break the British blockade of New York, had been launched. The *Demologos* was not, however, a sea-going vessel and sail had still a long way to go.[6] Britain looked on the advance of steam propulsion with anxiety, fearing that it might weaken the ascendancy at sea which she had acquired. Space does not

[5] Mahan, *The Life of Nelson*, p. 719.
[6] Preston, Wise, and Werner, *Men in Arms*, p. 321.

I. The Opposing Fleets converge

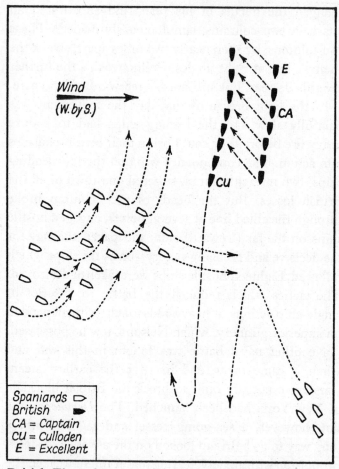

British Fleet, from double Column, form single.
Spanish Weather Division first running E.S.E.; three
    Ships pass across British Line and join Lee Division;
    the rest haul to the Wind and reach N. by E.
Spanish Lee Division on Port Tack, seeking Contact
    with Weather Division.
British ordered to tack and pursue Spanish Weather
    Division.

VINCENT: 14 February 1797
MAN ŒUVRE

II. Crisis of the Battle

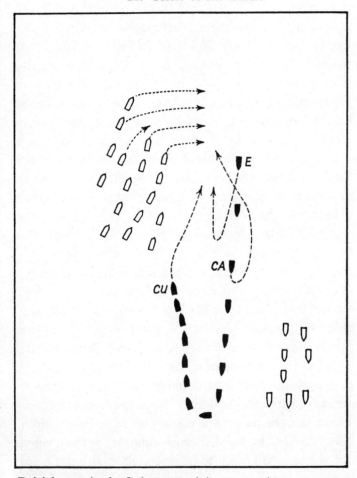

British, as single Column, tack in succession to engage
    Spanish Weather Division.

Spanish Weather Division turns E. to pass behind
    British and join Spanish Lee Division.

Nelson in *Captain* leaves Line to head off Spanish
    Weather Division.

Troubridge in *Culloden*, the leading Ship, joins and
    supports *Captain*.

Collingwood in *Excellent*, the rearmost Ship, tacks
    to support *Captain*.

suffice to deal with the tactics of the last years of sail, the pattern of which was created by the Napoleonic Wars.

It must be admitted that the Revolution in France played into British hands because it practically destroyed the fine body of French naval officers. As for the Spaniards, they had some of the finest designers and shipbuilders in the world, but their navy was starved. Fleets rarely put to sea and when in port were manned by skeleton crews, brought more or less up to strength in war by sweeping in pressed men from the streets and farms. At the Battle of Cape St. Vincent some of these unfortunates went down on their knees when ordered aloft, being more frightened of a yard-arm than of cannon-balls. The British also used pressed men, but a considerable proportion of theirs were seamen. The best hands in a warship were minor masters of the art of war. The skill, coolness, and pluck of a captain of the top in a well-manned two-decker, such as those of the fleet trained by Jervis in the Mediterranean, made an invaluable contribution to victory. A petty officer of this sort merits the name of artist as well as that of man of mettle.

It has been mentioned, when dealing with strategy, that a nation with a predominant navy could shift its armies where it would and if necessary avoid places where the enemy's were present in superior strength. Nevertheless, forced landings—that is, against active opposition—had often to be undertaken. Britain, being unable to brave Napoleon on land without allies in the main theatres of war, and suffering from the fact that her allies were constantly being defeated and compelled to come to terms, undertook many forced landings. Some were spoiled by mistakes; some were rendered fruitless because, though the troops established a footing ashore, they could not maintain it; some were directed against objectives unprofitable in terms of the effort involved, however successful they might be. They were, however, an admirable means of waging war in the circumstances outlined and frequently very well conducted.

An example of the experts in amphibious operations generally is Admiral Lord Keith, who, on the other hand, never had the good fortune to take part in a purely naval engagement. He was concerned in the capture of Charleston in the American Revolutionary war, for which he was warmly commended, and in command of the expedition of 1795 which captured the Cape of Good Hope, for which he was raised to the peerage. After an abortive attack on Cadiz, for the botching of which he must take a share of the blame, he commanded the Egyptian expedition of 1801. It was no better equipped than its predecessors had been, which is not saying much. The commander of the troops, General Sir Ralph Abercromby, wrote: 'I never went on any service entertaining graver doubts of success.'[7] Since he had rarely enjoyed any success throughout his long career the outlook was ominous.

Some earlier ventures of this type had failed purely and simply for lack of consideration and training. Admirals and generals realized the need of training for their own forces, but not often that amphibious warfare called for it more urgently still, because the two services

[7] Lloyd, *The Keith Papers*, Vol. ii, p. 230.

participating lived and fought in different worlds and found it hard to understand each other's problems. We have no means of knowing whether it would have troubled Keith to undertake this difficult landing against French troops, and dependent on the capture of the fortress of Alexandria and its harbour, without rehearsal. However, when an opportunity occurred by chance he seized it. The expedition was held up in Marmarice Bay, north of the island of Rhodes, during negotiations with the Turkish authorities.

Keith put his marines at Abercromby's disposal. He placed one of his captains, Sir Alexander Cochrane, in charge of the disembarkation, and after pointing out to Abercromby that his ships of war were short-handed and the troopships even more so, pledged himself to do his utmost, not only for the landing but for the provision of supplies, ammunition, and stores. He then carefully rehearsed the procedure. The final plan was for the fleet to stand seven miles out to sea to cover the operation and the transports to move a couple of miles further in. From there a flotilla of boats and launches was to advance in three waves: 58 boats carrying 2,900 troops in the first, 90 boats carrying 2,700 in the second, the field artillery in the third. Two little bomb-ships and three sloops were simultaneously to engage Aboukir Castle and some blockhouses manned by the French.

As is well known, the landing on these lines was carried out with dauntless courage by seamen and troops alike. It was the first step leading to the surrender of the whole French Army in Egypt after a campaign in which there was hard fighting only during the first fortnight.

Had it not been well organized it must have failed. The victory aroused pride and an upsurge of confidence. 'We have beat them without cavalry and inferior in artillery. This is the Army of Italy!' wrote John Moore delightedly. The sentiment was re-echoed round the country.

One must conclude with the reflection, even though it be an anticlimax, that, had Bonaparte not gone home or Kléber not been murdered, there could have been no landing because there would have been four or five times as many troops to oppose it. As of Fuentes de Onoro in the Peninsular War, one must say: 'If Boney had been there we'd have been beat.'

Chapter Three

THE NINETEENTH CENTURY AND THE DEVELOPMENT OF MISSILES

THE nineteenth century was the happiest in human history from the point of view of the humanity with which its wars were waged. After 1815 it was not prolific in great wars. The first half was indeed remarkably free from wars between European powers. The causes of the long period of comparative peace after the Battle of Waterloo were manifold, most of them natural and laudable, but some less pretty below the surface. First comes sheer weariness of slaughter and remembrance of the losses of almost unceasing fighting over a generation ending in 1815. Allied with this sentiment was the growth of idealism or liberalism. Those who professed this faith detested war itself and for itself, not merely because it brought death and suffering or because they had in their minds memories of wars particularly bloody. They were strong in most European countries. The leader and ruler of one, the Emperor Alexander I of Russia, was an enthusiastic idealist. He was even inspired by the belief that he had a mission to liberalize his era, though by no means at the expense of Russian power or of his own authority over his people, which was absolute. Idealists often think on these lines, but we notice it most in emperors.

Another feature favouring peace was the habit of

holding periodical international congresses, the fashion for which had been set by the most famous, that of Vienna. However, the old obstinacy returned and the ambitious plan of maintaining peace by means of a succession of congresses had to be abandoned owing to irreconcilable differences of views. From congresses, however, was born a conception, somewhat vague to us but familiar and more real in the last century, the 'Concert of Europe'. It is briefly dismissed in an able book on the history of warfare with the comment that it 'had no great permanent value as a check on war in the nineteenth century'.[1] Once in a while able men write nonsense. If the world had ever found a permanent check on war there would have been little, if any, thereafter. The Concert of Europe was beneficent, so far as it went.

The same work echoes the belief frequently expressed by historians that one force, the British Royal Navy, made certain kinds of war virtually impossible. Not all kinds, of course, nor even all considerable wars. It did not stop the Austro-Prussian War of 1866 or the Franco-Prussian war of 1870, and no one in his senses had dreamt that it would or could. They were, in fact, wars in which sea power played no part to speak of, though the first of them produced one of the great naval figures of the century in the Austrian Tegethoff. The claim is that the strength of the Royal Navy and the policy of the United Kingdom made unlikely any approach to a European hegemony. The British Navy assuredly twice saved Turkey from Russian

[1] Preston, Wise, and Werner, *Men in Arms*, p. 197.

designs, first indeed by its part in the Crimean War,
but on the second occasion, in 1878, by its preparedness
and its presence on the scene. Earlier, in 1860, it had
stretched neutrality just as far as this would go in
covering the operations of Garibaldi against the
Bourbon Kingdom of the Two Sicilies. On occasion
its activities were imperious, if not arrogant. In 1850
it blockaded Greek ports in the role of process server
in an action for debts due to Don Pacifico, a Gibral-
tarian Jew and thus a British subject.

Another potent influence is to be found in the fact
that the powers with more or less absolute governments, Prussia, Russia, and Austria-Hungary, had got
out of the war that they wanted and did not desire to
risk it. They were more concerned with maintaining
the *status quo* than with expansions at each other's
expense. Fear of France was over and Napoleon died
at St. Helena in 1821. The spirit of the Revolution—
and even as Emperor he had been a man of the Revolution—had not, they had reason to know, died with
him. There was too much of it for their liking in their
cities, often allied with nationalism. It seemed likely
that war between the powers would be a forcing ground
for radicalism, Jacobinism, and sedition. Better when
possible to keep the peace, at the same time taking
care that the armies were ready for emergencies.

On the other hand, the fourth victorious power, the
United Kingdom, refused to subscribe to the doctrine
of the despotic states that revolution, however dig-
nified in form and however glaring the evils against
which it fought, should be attacked wherever it reared

its head. On the contrary, first Castlereagh then Canning resisted this principle strongly. And once more the Royal Navy in the background made everyone listen to what they said.

Two risks of a reversion to a warlike atmosphere were always present. That most likely to become a reality was the temptation for great powers to forget their long tradition of caution and to exploit for their own aggrandizement the changes taking place in European society, such as the demand of Christian populations for freedom from the Turkish yoke or of northern Italy to be quit of Austrian rule. The biggest single factor of this kind was the rivalry between Austria and Prussia for leadership of the German peoples. The second danger seemed more remote. It was the appearance of a new adventurer controlling the destinies of a great power. This actually happened —and to make matters worse the name of the upstart was Napoleon.

Meanwhile armaments were making considerable progress during the relatively peaceful first half of the century. The rifle, used in fair numbers by Americans in the Revolutionary War, was being established as the standard weapon, though in the Crimean War the Russian Army was mainly armed with smooth-bores. Rifling and the later development of loading at the breech instead of at the muzzle in both portable fire-arms and cannon is an example of how implements, for war as well as for peace, may be designed, tried, abandoned because too far ahead of contemporary resources, perhaps forgotten altogether, and finally brought forward again and established. So an extremely primitive cannon of the early fifteenth century was breech-loading, and in at latest the sixteenth the simplest form of rifling with straight grooves appeared.[2] Yet the principle of rifling did not become universal till more than half-way through the nineteenth century, and the British, having been among the pioneers of the breech-loading gun, were still using a muzzle-loader for horse and field artillery in the 'eighties. In the Austro-Prussian War the Austrians used muzzle-loading rifles and the Prussians breech-loading. In the Franco-Prussian War both sides were armed with breech-loading rifles.

The second half of the nineteenth century witnessed a vast development in missile weapons. This was a missile age. It changed the nature of tactics and the character of battles. The details must be briefly stated, in simple terms. Take cannon first. Their transformation was due not to a single or even several inventions but to rapid and continuous improvement in a number of respects. The gun itself, instead of being cast, was made of wrought iron and finally of steel. Grooving of barrels gave way to rifling with twisted grooves imparting spin. To make the gun stand an increased charge, it was wrapped with wrought-iron bands from the trunnions (the projections which rested on the carriage) to the breech. With stouter guns more powerful propellents could be employed, and by 1861 one was made available in the form of nitro-glycerine. The other type of explosive used by artillery, the charge in the shell,

[2] Carman, *A History of Firearms*, pp. 21, 105.

was also increased in violence. Fuses were made more reliable. And towards the end of the century the shock of the recoil was checked by a hydraulic or hydro-pneumatic buffer or brake-cylinder, which immensely increased the rapidity of fire. One example of increased range is found in the German field gun: 4,000 yards at the maximum in 1870 and 7,000 only three years later.[3]

In the portable weapon there was a similar series of improvements: rifling, breech-loading, brass-covered cartridges, smokeless powder, magazines feeding a fresh cartridge into the breech as the shell of the last fired was ejected, all combining to produce greater speed and accuracy, while troops behind cover were no longer betrayed by smoke as in the days of black powder. Fast as the rifle advanced in all respects, however, it was rapidly caught up and eclipsed by the machine gun, which, starting as a clumsy weapon of several barrels fired by turning a handle, became automatic, the mechanism being actuated by the recoil of the barrel or a portion of the gases of the cartridge.

These weapons were naturally in themselves more deadly than the old ones, but they tended at first to produce less result than short-range firearms in battles fought at close quarters. Battles now started at longer ranges; concealment began to be practised; infantry not in movement lay down; they could use breech-loaders while remaining prone; the foremost advanced by short rushes and the supports in companies or platoons spread out chequerwise in what became known

[3] Falls, *A Hundred Years of War*, p. 69.

as artillery formation. In the greatest engagement of the Franco-Prussian War, the simultaneous Battles of Gravelotte and Saint-Privat, the Prussian commanders, though they had long led troops armed with breech-loading rifles, had not yet faced troops in possession of them—still less with the primitive machine gun known as the *mitrailleuse*—in a battle on a vast scale. They were unprepared for the terrific effect of the fire of infantry. Their reaction was to make the final advance in loose skirmishing order, which led to spreading out, wider frontages, and increased efforts to turn the flanks of an enemy on the defensive.[4] The effect of defensive rifle fire in the American Civil War had to be learnt all over again because neither the Germans nor the French had paid it close attention.

Parallel with this growth in the power, range, and general efficiency of missile weapons was an increase in the speed and capacity of transport. This was due in part to the improvement in roads, in which two Britons, John Macadam and Thomas Telford gave a lead to Europe. The most striking factor was, however, the railway. Some early detailed evidence comes from the Crimean War.

The British ran a five-mile railway from Balaclava to their battery positions. Its lay-out appears ludicrous, an engineer's nightmare, but the ground was very difficult and the equipment primitive. A locomotive hauled the train over the first two miles; then a stationary engine hauled it, eight wagons at a time, up an incline so steep that the locomotive could not mount it;

[4] Maurice, *The System of Field Manœuvres, passim.*

next six horses pulled the wagons in pairs; then, over two gullies, the wagons ran singly by the force of gravity down one side and up the other; finally, horses took over again for the last stage. During the bombardment preceding the fall of Sevastopol this astonishing contraption brought up 700 tons of ammunition a day. It was looked on at the time as 'rather a marvel', though only two miles of the five were covered by what we regard as railway transport.[5] Haulage by horses of trucks on rails had been employed for military purposes much earlier.

The railway was in the main a strategic instrument, that is to say, it was used for mobilization, reinforcement, supplies and stores, and in general well out of reach of the enemy. Yet it could on occasion be used tactically also, and the Austrians employed it thus at Magenta in 1859.[6] A famous instance is that of the First Battle of Bull Run in the American Civil War. Confederate troops, marching straight into action after detraining from the Manassas Gap Railway, decided the issue. Strategic moves carried out by both sides were remarkable for the numbers of troops and the distances involved. This war has indeed been called 'a railway war'. It was the first in which engineer officers and civilian experts applied themselves scientifically and successfully to the adaptation of railways to the needs of war. In the Austro-Prussian and Franco-Prussian Wars of 1866 and 1870 railways were used on a very large scale. Over captured Austrian track the Germans used a train manned by engineers

[5] Luard, *Field Railways*.   [6] Ibid.

and pioneers, carrying rails and other plant for a permanent way, including some bridging material.[7]

At the same time the industrial revolution and a less complete but none the less important agrarian revolution were also exercising an effect on warfare. The former enabled weapons not merely to be improved, as has been shown, but to be turned out faster and in greater numbers. It produced facilities not originally intended for military purposes but useful in that sphere. To take a single example, the preservation of meat in sealed tins, first used on a big scale in the American Civil War, was a powerful aid to mobility and economy in weight and bulk. It has even been called in a pardonable hyperbole as important as the invention of gunpowder. The two revolutions were accompanied by another change to which they contributed greatly, the rapid growth of population.

So we see a number of interlinked factors working simultaneously to influence war: industry, invention, improvement in transport, and growth of population. One may add the electric telegraph, which made practicable the control of larger forces, though not their tactical leadership, which had to await the field telephone and was not established until the twentieth century. So armies, which had tended to shrink after the Napoleonic Wars, expanded again, eventually, under systems of conscription, to become larger than the biggest the Emperor had ever commanded. And since it was impossible in peace to maintain armies anything like as great as those to be used in war, the

[7] Luard, *Field Railways*.

conscripts were given a relatively short term of embodiment and training in the active army and then passed into the reserve, with the liability to be called back to the colours in the event of war.

In their turn these developments led to the transformation of military staffs. Some would have it that the word 'invention' should be used rather than 'transformation', but this belief betokens lack of historical sense and even of elementary imaginative faculties. It must surely be obvious that commanders such as Alexander, Hannibal, Caesar, could not have controlled their considerable armies as they did without the aid of lieutenants who deserve to be called staff officers. In the Napoleonic Wars the Prussian and Austrian staffs made striking progress in precision and objective thinking. Scharnhorst, Gneisenau, and Radetzky were remarkable chiefs of staff. Napoleon has been justly reproached with allowing his staff little scope because of his passion for keeping everything in his own hands. Yet his *aides-de-camp-généraux* were in fact high-grade staff officers. Bold and experienced, hard riders and well mounted, they could be relied on to transmit the spirit as well as the letter of verbal orders. On occasion they would even issue an order in the Emperor's name, based on their knowledge of his ideas.

A more thorough instrument of control was, however, obviously needed from the middle of the nineteenth century onwards, not only by the commander in the field but by the State itself. To handle armies increased in size and which the railways could deploy and supply on wide frontages some of the burden hitherto borne by the commander-in-chief had to be lifted. But first these great national armies had to be mobilized and put into the field as speedily as possible. Mobilization involved always the recall of the reservists and their fitting-out, but also the issue of equipment and transport. General staffs, aided by the yearly increase in the railway network and improvement in its management, shortened the period and continued to do so. In 1866 the Prussian Army took five weeks to mobilize and deploy against Austria. In 1870 it mobilized and was transported to the Rhine in eighteen days. In 1914 a British battalion stationed at Plymouth and with its depot, from which the reservists had to travel, at Aberdeen, some 480 miles away as the crow flies, received mobilization orders on the afternoon of 4 August and landed in France on the 14th.[8]

Apart from mobilization, over and done with as soon as it was completed, the functions of a General Staff were planning, operations, administration, discipline and promotion, intelligence (with counter-espionage probably included in the directorate), and training. Other departments such as weapons, supply, medical services, chaplains, education and welfare were eventually hived off. The man more than any other responsible for this extended staff system was Helmuth von Moltke, the elder. He stamped the German General Staff with his personality and ideas, and the German pattern's success made it the prototype, though other countries did not imitate it in all respects.

[8] Falls, *The Gordon Highlanders in the First World War*, p. 2.

'What Moltke sought above all was a standard of training which would guarantee that any senior officer of the General Staff would, when confronted by a given set of circumstances, take approximately the same action as any other. This necessitated not only careful training but also a thorough grounding in a common doctrine. . . . The railways had widened the areas over which armies operated and increased their size. . . . In consequence, it was more than ever necessary to insure that when men were "on their own" they should act according to a known pattern and not cause misunderstanding by eccentricity. The method sounds pedestrian, but its effects were in practice prevented from becoming harmful by the boldness universally enjoined.'[9]

For mass armies the control of marches was essential. It applied not only to the number of roads to be used, but also to the composition of the columns, in particular the position of artillery in them. It is obvious enough even to the layman that an advanced guard might be very badly knocked about if, on colliding with the enemy, there were no artillery, or very little, in a position to support the infantry and cavalry. But this consideration applied on a bigger scale than that of advanced guards. In the war of 1866 the Germans were constantly outgunned by the Austrians because their artillery marched too far back in their columns and, when contact with the enemy brought about a halt, found itself blocked. They did not repeat this mistake when they marched to meet the French in 1870. Nor

[9] Falls, *A Hundred Years of War*, p. 62.

did they allow batteries to become separated from their
wagons, as had happened in Bohemia. In the French
war a wagon followed each gun on the march and the
ammunition in the limber-wagon attached to the gun
was treated as a reserve.[10]

Some variation occurred in the methods of the
military nations. The French General Staff system did
not differ markedly from the German in theory, but it
did in practice. The initiative of staff officers was less.
One reason for this was doubtless the Napoleonic
tradition, under which the general kept all he could in
his hands. Another was that the highest German commanders were the King, the Emperor, and royal princes
who were nursed by exceptionally good staff officers
and in practice had to delegate a large amount of responsibility. (It must be recalled that the elder Moltke's
appointment was nominally never higher than that of
Chief of the General Staff.) France began the war of
1870 with the Emperor as ostensible Commander-in-
Chief, but staff officers never attained in time of war
the power of their German contemporaries. The
Austrians made their staff corps a closed body but
reconstituted it at intervals. The British did not form a
General Staff until between 1903 and 1905. The interpretation of some ignorant commentators has been that
there was no British staff work. What was in fact
lacking was systematic staff work on the principle that,
though a General Staff consisted of a group of individuals doing different jobs, the staff was a unity co-
ordinated by one man.

[10] Hohenlohe-Ingelfingen, *Letters on Artillery*, pp. 52, 111.

Let us look at four examples of the new generalship: Radetzky, Lee, Grant, and Moltke. The first was a general of the Napoleonic Wars whose astounding retention of mental and physical powers carried him as an octogenarian into the intermediate period. He manœuvred brilliantly at Novara, but his victories and great marches do not fully represent the new warfare of forces running into hundreds of thousands, of railways, the telegraph, and the modern General Staff. From this point of view Radetzky is most interesting in his forward-looking and acute studies of military factors, from world politics to the mounting of cavalry. Poland will be the advanced guard of 'the great northern colossus' (Russia); India will free herself from Britain, despite the asset of a canal from Suez to the Mediterranean—the first prophecy looking nearly a century ahead, the second well over a century ahead and the third forty years. The United States will become the supreme world power—this in 1829.[11] As early as 1811, when Austria was at peace with Napoleonic France, Radetzky opened the first administrative staff course in Vienna. And at the other end of the scale this cavalryman interested himself intensely in veterinary science, stud farms, equitation and *dressage*, breaking and training, feeding, grooming and shoeing.[12]

It was a tragic error on the part of Jefferson Davis, the President of the Confederacy in the American Civil War, not to have appointed Robert E. Lee Commander-in-Chief until at least two years too late and only a

[11] Regele, *Feldmarschall Radetzky*, pp. 204–6.
[12] Ibid., pp. 400, 404–9.

few weeks before he had to surrender at Appomattox Court House. The contention of some good writers on the war that, despite his finer intellect, he did not see it as a whole as clearly as Grant, remains unproven. The best writer of all points out that Lee could only suggest or plead, but that during the short period in 1862 when he was the President's military adviser he showed fine gifts in large-scale strategy when he planned the redeployment of the forces and the moves between the Shenandoah Valley and Richmond.[13]

There was not much room for large-scale strategy on the side of the Confederacy because it started with the general aim of making the Union Government realize that the South was unconquerable. Thus its attitude was defensive, without broad projects. The Federals, on the other hand, started with strategy on a gigantic scale and of remarkable quality. The 'Anaconda Plan' involved naval blockade of the Southern ports; the opening of the Mississippi down to the Gulf of Mexico, which would cut away the Western States from the Confederacy and complete the eastern and southern naval blockade by a western blockade along the great river; and finally the crushing of the Confederacy as an anaconda or boa constrictor crushes its prey. This scheme, never formally adopted and on occasion thrust into the background, was none the less the basis of Federal strategy.

On the second plane of strategy, the operations of a large and often widely separated army, Lee was superb. He was an equally good tactician, with an unfailing

[13] Freeman, *R. E. Lee*, Vol. ii, pp. 7–16.

eye for the best defensive position available and for the places where hasty fortification would prove most effective. He also used the defensive locally in order to economize strength and 'to provide himself with a greater proportion to be employed in the open'.[14] He was perhaps the only one among the foremost generals of that war to recognize fully the power of the rifle. Most of them persisted in costly frontal attacks. They did not realize, on the other hand, that when frontal attack was necessary, the skirmishing line should be built up gradually to a strength sufficient to carry out the final assault itself instead of preparing it by fire and leaving its execution to assault columns. In the war against Austria which followed hard on the heels of the American Civil War the Prussian Army attempted to use columns thus, but these tended to merge into the skirmishing line till both together formed one heavy line which launched a final charge from a distance as short as a hundred yards. This tactic was confirmed in the Franco-Prussian War. Afterwards it was embodied in the official doctrine of the majority of armies. The celebrated French historian and tactical theorist, General Colin, writes: 'The combat was transferred to the skirmishing line, which previously only prepared it'.[15] This method was used with great effect by the Japanese against the Russians in 1904 and 1905, though their assault was made from a greater distance. It was that of the early battles of the First World War, before trench warfare set in.

[14] Falls, *A Hundred Years of War*, p. 60.
[15] Cclin, *Les Transformations de la Guerre*, pp. 45, 88.

The second great commander of the Civil War, Ulysses Grant, owes his fame in part to his manœuvres and battles on or near the Mississippi; in part to his direction of the final campaign, brought about by his recognition of how the greatly superior strength and equipment of the North could be used to make victory certain. His plan was in brief to hold and grind down the main force of the Confederacy under Lee in Virginia and set free Sherman to move south into the enemy's deep rear. Grant's force was the heaving bodily might of the Union; Sherman's the swinging, long-reaching arm which was to destroy the Confederacy's railways, stores, and food, to reduce it to impotence by the use of the incendiary torch as much as by the weapons of war. The one practised naked attrition while his lieutenant practised wholesale slaughter of cattle and pigs and, in South Carolina, marched day after day under clouds of black smoke. Sherman himself believed that only about one-fifth of the destruction he wrought concerned the Confederate Army directly.

If we study Grant in 1863 at Vicksburg—his manœuvres to cut its communications with the east, then his establishment of a powerful force on the Mississippi below the town, his merciless investment covered from interference by a detachment under Sherman, the final surrender of an allegedly impregnable fortress and a garrison 30,000 strong—we learn something of the high art of war. If, on the other hand, we turn our eyes to the warfare of attrition practised by Grant against Lee in the Wilderness, we shall probably conclude that, great man though Grant was in his way, this was an example of a second-grade art of war. Grant's strategy was completely successful and may well have been necessary. Yet if, as his out-and-out admirers hold, it could not have been avoided, the deduction must surely be that with odds of two to one in his favour, Grant was incapable of winning an advantage over Lee by manœuvre.

Moltke is close to the highest type of German staff officer, but as commander-in-chief—which he was for practical purposes—the lightness of his control has rarely if ever been equalled by any soldier endowed with comparable gifts. He could afford to give subordinates their heads because the Prussian Army was far better trained than any other in the world. At the same time looseness of control was to some extent forced upon him by the breadth of the deployment of his forces. In 1886, against Austria, the original frontage was one of 260 miles. He drew up elaborate plans for deployment and approach marches, but held that, once contact with the enemy was established, the next plan must depend on circumstances. Since the Austrians, fighting with muzzle-loaders against breech-loaders, lost four times as many men as the Germans, even when the former scored a success, we may say that Moltke was bound to win that war.[16] His reputation must therefore rest largely upon his conduct of the campaign against France in 1870.

Here his plan, though fluid in time and space, was fixed in principle. He intended to manœuvre so as

[16] Fuller, *War and Western Civilization*, p. 108

always to be assured of superior strength and to attack the French at once, wherever they were found. His eye was always fixed on Paris because he believed its significance to be even greater than that of capitals in general. It has been said that his method was rather like that of a chairman of company directors, but at crises or when fresh directives were called for he intervened decisively and almost always to the best possible effect. He was very bold. Indeed, his boldness might have led him into the gravest trouble because of his habit of acting on assumptions when in doubt about the French movements, if his foes had been better led. Few commanders can have fought more battles which they did not intend to fight, or did not mean to fight in the way or at the time the battles occurred. Spicheren was fought owing to the indiscipline of a subordinate who collided with a French position without having any notion of how strongly it was held. Colombey was brought on by a brigadier. Vionville-Mars la Tour began with an attack by a dangerously isolated German corps on a force several times its own strength. The great twin battles of the war, Saint-Privat and Gravelotte, followed a highly speculative German advance begun in the erroneous belief that the French were in full retreat from Metz towards Verdun.

Moltke was at his greatest as an organizer. He seems to have felt, and indeed went far towards admitting, that when the new mass armies clashed accident was bound to play a big part, so that 'genius was subordinate to the offensive spirit'.[17] Yet it was not a

[17] Fuller, *The Decisive Battles*, Vol. iii, p. 134.

DIAGRAM III

FRANCO-GERMAN WAR: GRAVELOTTE-ST. PRIVAT, 18 AUGUST 1870

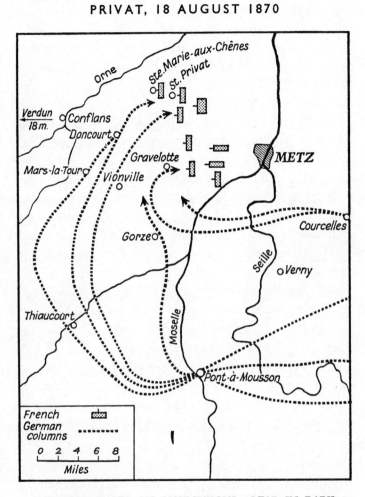

STRATEGY BASED ON ASSUMPTIONS—LEAP IN DARK

Thinking Bazaine has retreated towards Verdun, the Germans first run into the French at Vionville-Mars la Tour (Aug. 16). Next, unsure whether Bazaine has moved west or fallen back towards Metz, they push on northward, in fact exposing strung-out columns to flank attacks. Gravelotte-St. Privat is fought with both sides facing their own lines of communication, but decides the fate of the war.

blind offensive, even though he knew it was some-times overdone—he actually got rid of Steinmetz, the culprit at Spicheren, at the earliest possible moment. He knew the value of his artillery in both tactics and material. It was his prime battle-winner, just as railways were the instrument by which his great armies subsisted and moved.

We should not denounce his rigidity or his virtual dismissal of genius as an impossibility in the new kind of war without making an effort to understand the handicaps which this imposed. The railways and the well-organized supply trains enabled him to put a vast army into the field, to provide it plentifully with ammunition, and to feed it. On the other hand, control by the commander-in-chief became far more difficult than in the day of Napoleon I. The telegraph helped in mobilization and approach marches, but little or not at all in tactical marches or on the battlefield. For that the man on a horse had to carry the order. Moltke is a majestic figure of an era of transition.

'The successes are not to be denied, and stand among the greatest which history has recorded. The fact is that, in the absence of genius . . . a sound spirit and a sure doctrine were applied to the struggle.'[18]

[18] Foch, *De la Conduite de la Guerre*, p. 481.

Chapter Four

SMALL WARS

IN normal wars disparities in strength and arms occur often enough, but approximate equality is more usual. Sometimes it is startling. In the final land battle of the Russo-Japanese War, Mukden, the nearest figures for combatant strength are 310,000 on either side. On reflection, a tendency to something like equality will be found natural. In most wars neither side would have taken up arms without hope of victory; if one is considerably the weaker, it sees at least a fair chance of wearing down its foe or holding out in the expectation of outside support. There have been, however, in the period under review, many wars with different backgrounds: wars of despair wherein bands from beaten armies have fought on as guerrillas; wars waged by regular armies against primitive peoples, who do not calculate the prospects of victory or are too ignorant to calculate objectively; wars where the nature of the country, as in mountains, deserts, and marshes, the familiarity of the inhabitants with their country, and the relative clumsiness of an invader campaigning in it, help to make up for the former's inferiority in weapons and equipment.

The title of this chapter is one of significance to the British Army. It is that of a constantly consulted book by a British writer, Major-General Sir Charles Callwell.

So far as his study goes, it is invaluable, but there have been many developments since the publication of its last edition. These wars differ widely, but they can conveniently be divided into four groups, though features of one type often appear in another. First stands the commonest, war against primitive peoples, most often colonial wars. Next comes guerrilla revolt against a government, whether native or foreign. Then there is a kind common in Latin America, in which both sides are armed with up-to-date light weapons but virtually no heavy ones. The fourth is the most modern kind, entirely underground and secret warfare, sometimes using sabotage as its main weapon.

Until the present century the main tasks of the commander of regular forces in a colonial type of war were to keep his troops fed and still more to keep them on their feet. Improved means of transport and skill in the prevention and treatment of disease, especially tropical disease, somewhat altered the situation. Against martial peoples like the mountaineers of the North-West Frontier of India, the Zulus, and the Berbers, the enormous advantages conferred by superior weapons did not save regular troops from the risk of disastrous accidents. At Adowa, a considerable Italian force was overwhelmed by the Abyssinians, and the castration of the prisoners made this small war the most humiliating of modern times to the defeated Europeans. At Isandlwhana a British force was surprised by a Zulu impi, armed only with the throwing and the stabbing assagai but highly drilled and tactically adroit, and virtually all the whites were slaughtered.[1] At Anual in Morocco the Spaniards suffered a similar disaster. Left-wing commentators have scoffed at the reputations of men like Wolseley, who made them by opposing modern missile weapons to weapons of the iron age, but, whether or not colonial wars were unjust, they were not without hair-raising risks.

In warfare the first objective is commonly the enemy's main body, the second his capital. In this sort of warfare, however, while the natives remain more mobile than the regular troops opposing them, regulars generally found it impossible to bring irregulars to battle unless they wanted to swap blows. As for the capital, there might not even be one, and anyhow its loss was not likely to affect a primitive people as the loss of London or Paris would affect the United Kingdom or France. If the main body of the forces of a primitive people were brought to action against their will by the regular army of a colonial power, the probable explanation was either that the regulars were exceptionally well led, or that the leaders or the tribes were exceptionally stupid. In many cases the commander of a regular force engaged in such a war fell back on a third objective, that which the tribesman most valued, his cattle and sheep, his stored grain or flour. This is often to those who wage it an unpleasant kind of war, carried out with restraint where there exists a hope of recovering the friendship of the people against whom it is waged.

In all warfare the moral factor is weighty, but in

[1] Coupland, *Zulu Battle Piece*, p. 24.

hardly any other is it as important as in this sort. Any hint of anxiety acts as a tonic to primitive people. All the commanders who have been most successful in such affairs have been of the type of the Spanish O'Donnell, the English Roberts, and the French Galliéni, men with nerves of steel. They would permit no retreat at any point, even in circumstances where it would have been good tactics in normal warfare. Wolseley pointed out that even a halt to await provisions gave the enemy 'such renewed courage as to make him forget the success you have perhaps already achieved'. A bold and confident bearing counted almost as much as straight shooting.

Straight shooting took on a new meaning when, in the present century, peoples such as those of the North-West Frontier began to obtain large numbers of modern rifles. Hitherto they had been armed for the most part with muskets bought in bazaars, whereas in the Waziristan campaign of 1919 the Mahsuds possessed about 11,000 modern rifles. They were good shots at long ranges and patient in awaiting opportunities. In this campaign and in the Moroccan War of 1921 to 1934 approach marches by night became the general rule. Tactics were revised. The formation of a square with the baggage inside was abolished by fire power. Officers learnt to think on a bigger scale in mountain war because they had to protect columns on roads from fire at the range of a mile or more, whereas when the enemy had been armed with smooth-bores firing slugs protection up to a couple of hundred yards had sufficed.

The uninitiated may be helped to realize the significance of Mahsud marksmanship in good light in the Waziristan campaign from a story related by a well-known former officer of the Indian Army, Brigadier Sir John Smyth, V.C., then a brigade major. He was walking along the piquet line with two orderlies, when one of them, a Garhwali, froze in his tracks and motioned to him to take cover. It was primitive instinct, for there was nothing to be seen. However, after sweeping the ground with powerful glasses, the British officer caught sight of a single Mahsud, crouched behind a rock. He decided that it would be absurd to be held up by one man whom he judged to be at least 900 yards away and pushed on, despite the protests of the orderlies. Then came a distant report—and a sudden pain in his hand.[2] Men who could shoot like that and at the same time had tactical skill and bravery enough to cover an advance by fire from a flank and finally charge in, sword in hand, were exceedingly dangerous foes. Their fathers and grandfathers may have been as bold and fanatical, but they were incapable of creating similar risks.

Modern weapons were not the only factors in upsetting the relations between the military value of regular troops and that of semi-savages like the Mahsuds or more civilized but still primitive fighting men. In the Second World War the peoples of Asia noted two features in particular. They saw Indian troops and even the British battalions outfought and dominated by the Japanese. They realized too, that when the Japanese

[2] Smyth, *The Only Enemy*, p. 110.

had been finally overborne and routed in Burma the British victory had been gained with the aid of great superiority in numbers, between two and three to one, complete command of the air, and far stronger artillery. They did not con so closely events in the distant Pacific, particularly on Guadalcanal, where the Japanese, meeting the superb American Marines, were thoroughly beaten. Multitudes believed, however—and believe still—that Japan would not have been defeated but for the atomic bomb. This inspired them with new confidence when they faced or prepared to face European troops.

The second deduction drawn from this war was tactical, and even more pregnant than the first. It was the folly of fighting a regular war with irregular troops against regulars. The Moors who stood in battle array in 1860 to keep the Spaniards out of Tetuan lost the fight and the town as well. This was sheer stupidity, and they could have given their enemy infinitely more trouble by ambushes, raids, and guerrilla tactics in general. The Sudanese spearmen who assembled in dense masses at Khartum and charged Kitchener's Anglo-Egyptian army were playing into his hands. They were offering themselves to be slain in thousands by his artillery, machine guns, and rifles. They were inviting him to destroy their forces and ruin their cause in a single brief engagement.

And so the old methods of the Spanish guerrillas in Spain which had baffled Napoleon's marshals were learnt over again. The guerrillas did not fight pitched battles against the French. They made every march unsafe. They annihilated small parties. They cut off French supply columns and denied the resources of the country to the enemy. So deadly was their threat that an officer carrying a despatch to or from France required an escort of as much as 200 cavalry. This was the true art of war for men in their situation. On the other hand, it was ghastly in the extreme. It was waged with savagery by the irregulars, as is generally the case, and provoked, as is again usual, reprisals of almost equal barbarity, including the slaughter of the whole population of villages, followed by the consignment of these to the flames.

These tactics were also adopted in revolts against governments, even in highly civilized states. It is to be noted, however, that in the most civilized they were rarely dangerous except when an orthodox war was in progress unless suitable country, mountainous above all, was available. Even in the tremendous conflict of the Second World War, the resistance movement organized against the Germans in France hardly came into the open until after the allied landings. France was too densely populated, too well roaded, and criss-crossed too thoroughly by telegraph and telephone systems to give an active resistance any chance of survival against strong and mobile occupying forces. The one region where revolt was maintained for a long period by large bodies of men was the so-called 're-doubt of the Vercors', precisely because it was a tract of high-lying, thickly wooded, rough and broken country. The greatest successes of revolts—and when carried out against European nations virtually their sole successes in times of general peace—have continued to be won in mountains and desert or semi-desert. Among the most notable is the revolt against the French in Algeria. The rebels have been too wise to expose themselves to French fire as their ancestors did. When they have been mown down in the open it has been because French skill and mobility, greatly increased by the use of helicopters, have caught them there. This war has also on both sides lived up to the guerrilla tradition of cruelty and breaches of what are called 'the laws and usages of war'.

As the title implies, these proposed brakes on barbarism are of two kinds: agreements, especially the Hague Regulations and those sponsored by the International Red Cross at Geneva, and conceptions of restraint in action and behaviour generally recognized, though not having the force of international law. It must be realized that, though these laws and usages originate in the minds of benevolent and philanthropic individuals, they can be made effective only by governments and that governments cannot be expected to go out of their way to make things easy for rebels. Yet the laws and usages are often far from illiberal. For instance, absence of uniform does not necessarily deprive troops of the rights of combatants, even though forces not in uniform are a pest to regular armies because they can fight as soldiers and step back into the security of civil life on alternate days. However, though guerrillas may fight in civilian clothes without loss of combatant rights, they must at least wear a 'distinctive emblem' in order to retain them. In modern times they rarely do so continuously and would lose most of their efficiency if they did. In theory, if they break this rule their execution is justifiable. In practice, a number of officers, all on the defeated side, it need hardly be said, were tried and condemned after the Second World War by special tribunals and courts for such acts of reprisal. Governments supporting resistance movements—as they can nowadays effectively with the aid of wireless, aircraft, and submarines—ought to exercise care in the choice of instruments. They have not done so, any more than irregulars have worn distinctive emblems.

It may well be that the shocking deterioration in the conduct of war which has become a feature of our times has deprived the greatest and most civilized countries of moral sense and the moral right to act as judges of what is and what is not a breach of international law. Their own major weapons are described as indiscriminate, but in fact they are specifically designed to destroy the civil population, which includes women and children, not the fighting forces of their foes. The defence is the old one that necessity knows no law. 'Moral considerations (in the Second World War) were important only when they were also expedient.'[3]

If guerrillas attain great success in their type of war and can obtain arms on a large scale from neighbouring states, they may decide that it is worth while to go over to 'regular' warfare, wholly or partially. Two striking instances occurred after the Second World War. In Greece, which was bordered by three Communist

[3] Preston, Wise, and Werner, *Men in Arms*, p. 322.

states, Albania, Yugoslavia, and Bulgaria, the Communist rebels thrived for a long time on the support of these allies, who not only armed and fed them but even provided training camps, refuge in adversity, and hospitals outside the Greek frontier. Filled with confidence and pride as a result of their successes, the leaders of the 'Bandits' decided to fight the Greek Army in the open. Early in 1949 they launched a strong offensive on Florina. But by September they had been utterly routed and the pacification of the country had been completed. Ambition led to their downfall. They could certainly have maintained the fight for longer on guerrilla lines, though they realized that they had no hope of defeating the Greek Army and overthrowing the Government by those methods in view of the support given to it by the United States and Britain.

The second instance was the rebellion of Ho Chi Minh against the French in Viet-Nam. There too Communism and guerrilla warfare triumphed in the early stages, again with the aid of a neighbouring Communist state, in this case China. The arrival on the scene of an exceptionally able soldier, General de Lattre de Tassigny, exercised much the same effect as when General Papagos took over in Greece. De Lattre's victories, though mainly defensive, afforded France another chance. However, politicians and people were half-hearted about the war and such enthusiasm as was felt for it disappeared on de Lattre's death, only about a year after his appointment. It is therefore difficult to decide whether Ho Chi Minh and his generals were right in going over to warfare in which battles occurred with 50,000 men on either side fighting *coude-à-coude* in the Red River Delta. It is safe, however, to say that it practically never pays. It at once presents the regular forces of the enemy with the objective they have hitherto lacked, a concentrated body of troops to strike at.

The civil wars of Latin America stand by themselves by reason of the unreliability of the armed forces. Instead of serving as a guarantee of stable government —their main *raison d'être*, since wars between states are relatively rare—they have been responsible for countless revolutions. The commonest situation is that part of the army rebels and another part remains faithful. Occasionally the army takes one side and the navy the other, and now there are air forces to complicate matters. So we have professionals, and often intelligent ones, on both sides. In the majority of cases, however, the aim of a potential corrupt dictator to replace an existing corrupt dicatator has not been reckoned as worth the spilling of much blood, with the result that loyal forces and revolutionaries go through the motions of fighting and the issue is settled one way or the other in a very short time and with very few casualties. Yet South American peoples have a large vein of idealism and when their ideals take charge they fight fiercely. Some of their civil wars have been prolonged and bloody. In their wars of liberation two heroic figures, San Martin and Bolivar, immortalized themselves as great soldiers and patriots.

In the more serious of these wars tactical skill has

often been remarkably high, especially in the early days before urbanization had reached its present scale. The hardy country-folk were 'men who could shoot and ride'. Those who were not soldiers in the armed forces were often excellent natural soldiers, enduring, frugal, endowed with an instinct for the choice of ground and a highly-developed sense of direction by night as well as day. The tactical details and lessons of these wars have been little studied by Europeans, but they would surely merit closer attention.

Underground resistance in civilized and industrial countries is almost entirely new. The reason is that the times have been propitious to it. 'Total war' reached its fullest development in the middle of the Second World War. This was also a period in which Hitler's Germany had conquered and occupied a number of highly industrialized countries, the chief being France, Belgium, and Czechoslovakia. The industrial resources of these countries were exploited for Germany's war effort. In many cases the artisans were unwilling contributors to it. In Germany itself vast numbers of 'slave workers' had been brought in from occupied territories to the factories and arsenals of German war industry. It will be pointed out in a later chapter that total war depends on a complex and highly organized industrial development and that this is susceptible to sabotage which, when cleverly carried out, may be difficult to discover.

'The war effort depends on a chain of construction: basic industries, arsenals and armament factories, light industries making accessories, processing and finishing workshops, and the communications which link them together and convey the products to the armies. The whole constitutes a complex and vulnerable organization.'[4]

Sabotage undoubtedly caused the Germans trouble and involved losses in war production. Statistics are difficult to obtain, but it seems clear that in this country we exaggerated the effects of sabotage as, under the influence of propaganda, we exaggerated those of many other favourable factors. The Germans had an efficient system of inspection backed by ruthless and all-powerful security police. These in their turn were supported by similar organizations of Fascist sympathies in the occupied countries. Terror of the Gestapo, of the torture it employed in its interrogations, and of its frightful punishments, proved to be strong safeguards. Nevertheless, sabotage in war is a factor of increasing importance which can never be left out of account. Even in the armed peace of today it constantly occupies the attention of secret services.

Another feature of the Second World War which should not be forgotten is the fashion in which resistance movements were exploited by Communism. Here the fact that Soviet Russia, the ally which bore so much of the weight of the war, was Communist, had great influence. In Western Europe some of the Communist forces were at least as anxious to destroy their political foes as to fight Germans. The Second World

[4] Falls, *A Hundred Years of War*, p. 276.

War brought Communism enormous success and prestige in Western Europe, some of which it has since lost. When normal government was restored in France and Italy after the war the Communists sent a larger number of representatives to the parliaments of both countries than any other party.

In general military opinion in Britain inclines to the belief that support of resistance movements was over-done in the Second World War. Many of their adherents were men and women of the purest patriotism and the most sublime courage. Many who were caught were so handled that when death came finally it appeared as a release from a life which had become intolerable. Yet others of the Communist brand were not merely discreditable but dangerous allies. Their savagery employed against fellow-citizens, in France for example, left a legacy of hatred which afterwards poisoned society and only began to subside after nearly a generation. In the long run they damaged the interests of the country—nearly always the United Kingdom—which had backed them to an extent outweighing any services they may have rendered.

Among the most successful partisans of the war were the Russian. No moral objection can be taken to them. They were of the same blood as the soldiers, inspired by the same ideals, and fighting on the same soil, that of Russia itself. They were no concern of anyone except the Soviet Government—and the enemy. Yet even their exploits were almost certainly exaggerated. German writers have little to say about them,

except that they often cut railways.[5] The final opinion
—though it can be no more than that—is that partisans
of all kinds exercised less influence than has commonly
been asserted.

[5] A cursory re-examination of *Lost Victories* by Field-
Marshal von Manstein, to whom they must have been as
significant as to anyone, has revealed hardly a mention of them,
but the book is long and the index chiefly proper names and
units.

To read this bull
is to know why the Brits
suffered so...

Chapter Five

STRATEGY AND TACTICS OF THE FIRST WORLD WAR

THE war destined to be called the First World War began with an exploration of uncharted military ground. The last European war which could be described as 'great' had ended forty-three years earlier. The last 'big' war had been fought in the Far East, so far from European arsenals and depots of manpower that the European belligerent, Russia, had been unable to engage in it at full strength. Even in the decade which had elapsed since the latter war great changes in armament and equipment had occurred. A long list of questions difficult to answer assailed the most thoughtful minds. What was it going to be like? A few who had ruminated on the Russo-Japanese War thought that field fortification might play a leading part, though it is safe to say that none foresaw what entrenchment would amount to from 1916 onward. The few were not all soldiers. The man who possessed, or at least expressed, the clearest appreciation was a Polish banker named Bloch, who prophesied that stalemate would occur in the next war and that it would be a war of entrenchments. He was right about the entrenchments and right about a stalemate of long duration on the Western Front. There was, however, contrary to uninstructed belief, no complete stalemate anywhere else.

One lesson, the importance of artillery, was clear to all observers. However, the entrenchments of the Russo-Japanese War had been single lines and, since defence in depth by means of successive lines of trench was not foreseen, little emphasis was placed on heavy artillery. The small British Expeditionary force sent to France in August 1914 possessed hardly any. Such heavy artillery as was provided was expected to be useful mainly in the reduction of the permanent fortresses. It was to deal with these by high-angled fire that big howitzers had been designed. The most skilful and famous designer of the elaborate fortifications on frontiers and about great cities was the Belgian General Henri Brialmont. Three of his building, Lèige, Namur, and Antwerp, played a considerable part in the opening phase of the war. They were ring fortresses, that is a ring of forts about a central citadel, to keep hostile artillery from reaching it and the city. However, since they had been built, the range of super-heavy howitzers and the destructive power of their shell had greatly increased. None of the ring fortresses attacked could long survive once a strong siege train had come into action. Later on many of the fortress guns were removed for service in the field.

The introduction of reliable quick-firing field and horse artillery coincided with the opening of the twentieth century, and the types produced in the principal armies naturally tended to resemble each other closely. For example, the calibre of the French field gun was 75-mm. and that of the German 77-mm. The British equipments may be taken as a specimen, bearing in mind that the French 75-mm. had greater rapidity of fire, was slightly more accurate, and slightly less hard-hitting. The effective range of the 18-pdr. field gun was about 5300 yards and the maximum rate of *sustained* fire eight rounds a minute. An infantry division of 1914 was furnished, in addition to its 56 18-pdrs., with 18 4.5-in. field howitzers, the effective range being similar to that of the 18-pdr. and the maximum rate of sustained fire four rounds a minute.

The lessons of the South African War and the sensational performance of the French 'soixante-quinze' had led to searching of heart and constant discussion in the British Royal Artillery. How much risk should the artillery accept by using direct fire, which almost precluded cover and concealment, in support of the infantry? (It was ready to accept any, but sacrifice would be unprofitable if it resulted in the artillery being put out of action.) Was it correct tactics to follow closely the French theory of *rafales* (literally, squalls) of rapid fire to overwhelm resistance by sheer weight of shells, or should the British practice of slower, carefully ranged, bombardment of the most suitable targets be maintained?[1] Would counter-battery fire, which had gone out of fashion, recover its importance in a great war between first-class powers?

Solvitur ambulando. The war made cover and concealment necessities. After the early period of open warfare direct fire went out and did not reappear except occasionally in big battles until the front loosened

[1] Callwell and Headlam, *History of the Royal Artillery*, Vol. ii, pp. 44, 156, 193.

up again in 1918. Fire was controlled by a F.O.O. (forward observation officer) with a telephone, and after dark the guns were laid on 'night lines' in case of emergency. Attacks were made under barrages which jumped forward from trench to trench or objective to objective and from the Battle of the Somme in 1916 crept forward, so that all ground should be swept by fire. These barrages were gradually deepened till they became, instead of moving walls of fire, zones of fire several hundred yards in depth. This monstrous weapon was handled *usually not* with skill. For example, a barrage, having reached the limit of its advance, might *or might not* roll back to its start-line and then forward again, throwing the hostile infantry who had come into the open into confusion. Intelligence gathered from captured documents and prisoners was applied to artillery tactics. When the Germans at 'Third Ypres' in 1917 began to hold their counter-attack divisions well forward in order to avoid as far as possible the dreadful losses incurred in coming up through the British barrages, the Royal Artillery quickly caught on to the change and punished these divisions so severely that they had to be pulled back again. This too was speedily realized by the gunners, who then assailed them in their approach marches more effectively than ever, and, with the aid of the Royal Air Force, even in dead ground, so that their counter-attacks often petered out. Counter-battery work became so essential that special counter-battery staffs were formed.

Set programmes, however, made speedy tactical

improvisation difficult, and here progress was very slow. Telephone cable was constantly cut by fire and later on by tanks; wireless was primitive and did not extend sufficiently far forward, while portable sets did not pass the experimental stage. Thus demands for re-bombardment or a renewed barrage often failed to obtain a response or got it too late, and many opportunities were thereby lost. Pigeons achieved some marvellous successes but were unreliable. Flags displayed and flares lit by infantry and the old signal lamp had the obvious disadvantages. Coloured fireworks were probably, taking the war as a whole, the soundest method of tactical communication in the midst of a battle, though confusion resulted when both sides used them at once. The Germans employed them with great effect. The tremendous bombardments and barrages broke up the ground and seriously hampered the operations they were designed to support. Senior artillery officers recognized clearly that there was such a thing as 'over-bombardment', but they were not altogether their own masters in this respect.[2]

Demands for increased infantry fire-power led to the arming of battalions with light machine guns and small mortars. The heavier machine guns fired from a tripod were in the British Army then grouped in companies and eventually a battalion in each division. By the end of the war a division possessed seven times as many machine guns as at the start, and divisions which had not been reduced from twelve to nine battalions possessed nine times as many. The Germans

[2] Rawlins, MS.

and French made similar developments, but the less highly industrialized belligerents could not imitate them.

Fortresses and fire-power thus stood as question marks. In naval warfare the biggest was represented by the submarine. It was realized from the first that it would render the old system of close blockade virtually impossible; a warship would not dare to lie off a blockaded port in the submarine era. Britain determined to carry out a long-distance blockade of the ports of her foes. This was of doubtful legality and indeed characterized by Germany as piracy. Britain solved the problem by adding to the list of goods classified as contraband of war to make them liable to interception anywhere at sea. She thereby made herself unpopular with the sea-faring neutrals and especially her future ally, the United States, but the last-named, recognizing without admitting that some allowance should be made for the fact that Britain was fighting for her life, did no more than protest, and the others were incapable of doing more. The significance of the submarine was, however, far wider, most of all for Britain, a country unable to keep her people alive, much less to conduct a great war, unless she could maintain her maritime communications.

The aeroplane, making virtually its first appearance in war, was to begin with a means of reconnaissance only. Though some development was to be expected, few had any conception how great this would be in range, speed, and armament.[3]

---

[3] Sea and air warfare of the two World Wars are dealt with more fully in Chapters VII and IX.

The internal-combustion engine provided greater mobility. British *Field Service Regulations* laid down that the lorries of the supply columns had a maximum range of 45 miles, a double journey of 90 miles out and back. The range was increased to 52 miles by the horse-drawn divisional trains.[4] Only the rearward transport vehicles were, however, motorized. Wireless telegraphy and long-range telephony—though both were still capricious and liable to failure when most needed—improved the power of control over long distances, and the field telephone did the same thing for tactical control, with the reservations made above.

Economics were discussed more anxiously than at the outset of earlier wars. It appeared that the financing of armies on so great a scale might be ruinous. Some economists went so far as to believe that the expenditure involved had made a war of nations impossible or would quickly bring it to a stop. Germany was intensely eager to make the war as short as possible because, with a Navy inferior to Britain's, she doubted whether her continental resources would enable her to maintain a long one.

These and other problems made the future an object of speculation. They did not lessen the energy with which the great powers' forces began their operations. France, Germany, Russia, and Austria launched major offensives.

One curious feature of this war was that the whole opening phase—many will argue, the whole course and

[4] Falls, *France and Belgium, 1917*, Vol. i, p. 194.

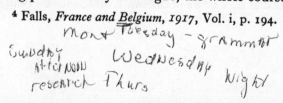

the result—was determined by a dead hand. Field-Marshal Count Schlieffen died eighteen months before the outbreak of hostilities and had given up his appointment as Chief of the General Staff of the German Army seven years earlier. His 'plan' was in fact a series of studies, the latest written in retirement and handed over to his successor, the younger Moltke. It was a plan contrary to the ideas of the recipient's famous uncle, who, as has been shown, disbelieved in detailed plans extending beyond the first collision with the enemy, yet it was in substance adopted by the nephew. In order to avoid running into the powerful French fortifications, Schlieffen's scheme was to violate the neutrality of Holland and Belgium—one of Moltke's emendations being to cut out Holland—and wheel forward with the main strength in the right wing, which was at the level of Paris to swing round the French array and drive the opposing armies either into neutral Switzerland or into the arms of the German armies in Lorraine. Meanwhile a relatively small army in East Prussia was to stand on the defensive against Russia and the rest of the task of holding back that Colossus would have to be left to the Austrians. Not for long, however. Within about six weeks, if the programme worked out right, the power of France would be broken and large German forces would begin to flow eastward over the well-organized railways to the aid of their allies.

The Schlieffen Plan has created much controversy. In the first place dispute has centred on the problem whether a cut-and-dried scheme founded upon an advance by the right wing of over 200 miles as the crow flies—much more as the troops marched—into the heart of France, against a foe outnumbered by about 12 per cent. only and less with the imperfectly trained Belgians counted, can be considered sound and practical. Further criticism has been directed against the apparent insouciance with which not Austria-Hungary only, but also East Prussia and even Silesia, were left open. Finally, it has been pointed out with some force that Schlieffen and his successor must have underestimated the speed with which the new factor of highly efficient railways would permit the French to move reinforcements from east to west along what would be the chord of an arc represented by the front when the German right wing approached the Seine.[5]

All this may be so. The fact remains, however, that the German plan did not fall far short of success and that its failure was due to weak leadership rather than to intrinsic defects. In its first phase the French were completely outmanœuvred and driven back to Paris and the Marne, without having suffered what could be considered proportionately heavy defeats in battle. In the second phase, the French counter-offensive, the Germans were equally outmanœuvred, without having suffered any serious tactical defeats, except in Lorraine.

The same thing is at least partially true of the first campaign in Galicia. There the outnumbered Austrians were much harder hit by the Russians than were the Germans by the French on the Marne, but two of

[5] Ritter, *The Schlieffen Plan*, pp. 6, 32.

their armies won fine victories. It was again manœuvre, the turning of the Austrian left by the Russian right, added to the strain of long fighting against heavy odds, that led to the deep Austrian retreat from Lemberg and Lublin. In East Prussia the Germans won a sensational victory at Tannenberg by manœuvre, a swift and secret concentration against the southern of the two Russian armies engaged.

Before going further let us glance at methods adopted to wage a war of nations, the doffing of coats and tightening of belts. Systems of control were not uniform but almost universal. Conscription was already in being in the continental countries and had only to be adapted to needs. In Britain it was introduced by slow stages and without enthusiasm. The economic structure was converted from a peace to a war basis, but again gradually; in fact in many instances the structure converted itself, Governments being content to expand the required industries by giving large orders to suitable firms or opening new works and allowing high wages to provide the incentive to the labour force. Food rationing followed a similar course, but became very severe in most countries. Taxation rose to a height which seemed incredible then, though most British taxpayers would be glad to go back to the scale now. Britain, with by far the biggest mercantile marine in the world—nearly half the world's ocean-going ships and more than half the tonnage[6]— exercised a very loose control of shipping to begin with. The Admiralty secured the power of requisition

[6] Salter, *Allied Shipping Control*, p. 7.

immediately, but used it only as required. Otherwise it hired, the shipowner finding the ship and paying wages at the level of peace and marine insurance, while the Government found the fuel, paid the balance of the increased wages, and bore the war risk. An indirect control was worked by measures such as prohibition or limitation of certain imports and refusal of licences to ships which carried coal out and returned in ballast.[7] This detail is given because it is interesting as an example of Britain's empirical approach to such problems, and will not be continued.

It was a railway war in a sense in which no other had been or was to be. For the forces of the Entente the railways were immensely important. It was customary, for example, for a separate train to carry supplies to every division in France each day, and this was exclusive of ammunition. During the planning for support to Italy in case of defeat by Austro-German forces the French railways promised sixty-two trains a day.[8] It was Germany, however, that obtained most from the railways. Throughout the war large bodies of troops were constantly passing to and fro between the eastern and western theatres. As a general rule they moved far quicker by rail than Britain and France could transfer them by sea to the eastern Mediterranean.

The course of the war in the west was one of rapid movement until October 1914, followed by a long period of stagnant warfare during which the changes in the front were hardly visible on small-scale maps.

[7] Salter, *Allied Shipping Control*, pp. 25, 26, 44, 50.
[8] Falls, *The First World War*, p. 287.

To say the least ✗

The Entente was generally on the offensive; indeed in 1915 the enemy was incapable of a prolonged major offensive because General von Falkenhayn transferred the major German effort to Russia with the object of aiding his Austrian allies to cripple her. The one big sustained German offensive was at Verdun in the first half of 1916. All the French and British offensives had been bloody and disappointing, and this was to be true of Verdun. From the point of view of the art of war the spectacle is uninspiring. And yet many senior officers were not men of high intelligence. Some showed what they could do in mobile warfare when they moved to more loosely-held fronts. One can imagine an army commander answering a critic thus: 'You say I should seek surprise, move my immediate supports in small columns instead of heavy lines, exploit success instead of hammering away at points where there have been failures, and generally introduce more manœuvre. All these ideas are commonplaces. How am I going to achieve surprise when we have scores of miles of wire to cut and hundreds of battery positions and machine-gun posts to deal with, taking several days? Then, whatever success we have in fire for destruction, there is going to be a German artillery barrage when we advance and—more serious —a great deal of fire from machine guns which are far harder to deal with than the artillery and in many cases impossible. So I must keep the infantry closed up and get it over the ground most heavily beaten by fire, which is no-man's-land, just as quickly as it can be done. Exploiting success? Manœuvre? We do all

DIAGRAM IV

FIRST WORLD WAR: ORGANIZATION OF A BRITISH BOMBING ATTACK

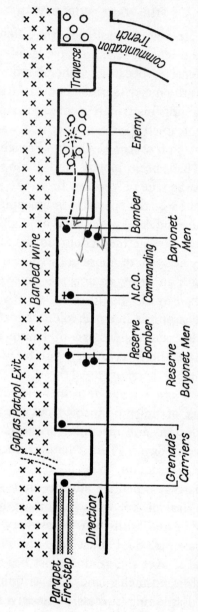

Bomber throws grenade over traverse: as it bursts, bayonet men dash round to attack the Enemy in the next Bay. Three or more parallel trenches might be attacked simultaneously.

we can to teach minor tactics in schools, and when divisions come out for training, I spend half my time as a preacher. But in this kind of warfare it is very hard for officers to find out even what is happening, let alone to take control of battalions or companies scattered all over the place. And remember we have got practically an army of amateurs now, and their fighting life is in trenches. The one thing they do magnificently is to clear a trench with grenades, and now that we have good rifle-grenades and hand-grenades trained British bombers will beat the Germans *not necessarily* nine times out of ten. But the trench is their world.'

The apologia may not be sound everywhere, but it contains a large measure of truth. Eventually surprise was rendered possible. For the British and French the tank was a factor—though it hardly became so until it had been in use for well over a year—because it could open gaps in the wire and thus enable preliminary bombardment to be eliminated or cut down to a minimum. Indeed, it was found possible to do without even previous registration of fire and to engage hostile batteries by the map, after finding them by air photography or by two ingenious systems of identification, 'sound ranging' and 'flash spotting'. The Germans produced only a handful of tanks. Their speciality in the offensive was the use of a mass of powerful and well-handled mortars which they concentrated on the foremost defences and by means of which they eventually cut down preliminary bombardment to under three hours, a time short enough for full strategic surprise. The remark about grenades refers to tactics

often used, slow and limited in scope, but commonly
~~not~~ costly in human lives.

In the other theatres of war conditions and equipment varied, but in none were the troops so numerous
in relation to the extent of the front as in France and
Belgium. Tanks were never used anywhere else, except
for a few in Palestine. By far the most important, after
the French front, was the Russian. In May 1917 the
fatal month in which the Government invited the
Soviet to join it, the number of divisions of the Central
Powers in Russia was precisely the same as that of the
German divisions in France and Belgium, 141 in each
case, but on a front upwards of twice as long. Entrenchment was more primitive and heavy artillery
not nearly so strong. As a result a break-through was
more readily attainable and the fluctuations of the front
were frequent and sometimes immense. Generally
speaking, though in all theatres of the war entrenchment was used and phases of deadlock occurred, deep
and rapid offensives took place. Of the outer theatres
of war the Macedonian campaign was fought largely
on French initiative and Palestine wholly on British.
Mesopotamia was British also, but carried on by the
Government largely against the view of the War
Office. The campaign in the Caucasus was a self-
contained struggle between Turkey and Russia. The
attempt to force the Dardanelles, promising strategically, failed within the space of a year. Italy was nearly
overwhelmed in 1917 but the Austrians collapsed
quickly in the final Italian offensive of 1918.

The powers concerned, France, Britain, Germany,

Austria, and in the final stage America, all regarded the Western as the principal front where the issue would be decided. This fact, in the circumstances outlined, made a prolonged and ferocious struggle in that theatre inevitable. It was a conflict of wills as well as of material. The victory was in fact won in the west and though the armistices with Bulgaria and Austria were signed before that with Germany in the Forest of Compiègne, it was the defeat of Germany in the west that broke the strength of the Central Powers.

The Revolution and military collapse in Russia gave Germany her third chance to win the war. The first had been lost on the Marne in 1914, the second by the defeat of the submarine offensive in 1917. German divisions poured across the continent until the total reached 208 in the spring of 1918, an increase of sixty-seven within a year. A series of five great offensives, one a month from March to July, were launched with the force of thunderbolts. The Entente's defence wavered dangerously, though some resolute men were always at hand to stave off utter rout when it seemed to be impending. The first arrivals among the American divisions also brought an unwearied spirit and high courage to the encounter. Tactically the offensive was a triumph for German skill and determination, but the director, General Ludendorff, was a tactician only and the huge pockets created did not bring strategic gains in proportion to the effort. This effort also put the finishing touch to the attrition which the Germans had already undergone.

When the first counterstroke was delivered on the

Marne on 8 July a big American army was beginning to reach France, and, though relatively few divisions could be put into battle for some weeks more, this growing and spirited reserve was a great asset. There can be no doubt, however, that the major factor in the victory of 'the hundred days' was the army of the British Empire or that the British Commander-in-Chief, Field-Marshal Sir Douglas Haig, was the dominant national leader. The Frenchman, Marshal Foch, had saved the allies from defeat, but Haig's role in victory was greater even than his. His troops responded marvellously to his demands upon them.

Since the advance was on an immense front and the Germans avoided a break-through by wholesale abandonment of ground whenever penetration looked likely, tactics were largely confined to the handling of tanks, artillery, and infantry, to village fighting—in which the troops showed unexpected skill after the years of trench warfare—and to proficiency in the speedy bridging of rivers and canals. It may be doubted whether Haig was a great tactician, except in defence, but he was a great soldier. In tactics he often deferred to the ideas of his army commanders, but there was never any question about who was master. In adversity as well as in victory he maintained the Army's confidence and trust.

Chapter Six

THE QUEST FOR PROTECTION

BEFORE recorded history, man, giving vent to his rage or greed, ceased to confine himself to striking blows or throwing stones. At some early stage he discovered that a primitive wooden shield, carried in one hand, did not interfere with the use of a club in the other but afforded cover to his head and body. Long years after first using a sword he fixed a guard below the hilt to save his hand. He found that a tough leather jerkin kept out most cuts and thrusts. When bows and slings came in he found the shield more valuable than ever, and improved it. When the art of Tubal Cain, that of working metals, became widespread, man began to armour his person, his horse, his chariot. He put stakes or a wattle fence round his hovel and went on to build stone walls about his house, his village, and finally his city. The search for shelter has never ceased.

The nineteenth century had been described as one notable for the development of missile weapons. Consideration of this phase in the abstract would lead us to suppose that the search would be for protection against weapons of this type, and this was actually the case. In some instances, as in that of gun and armour in warships, there was a continual conflict, a race to keep ahead in efficiency. It was a complex struggle

because the gun, designed to pierce armour, at the
same time required the protection of armour in its
barbette or turret. After the launch of the *Gloire* by
the French in 1859,[1] armour plating went up from
four to five inches; the first gun-turret was tested
successfully by the British Admiralty and both British
and French guns were strengthened by wrought-
iron bands from breech to trunnions to enable them
to stand higher charges. Passing on into the next
century, we find a similar process in land warfare.
The tanks first exploited in 1916 were impervious to
bullets. Before long, however, the Germans introduced
armour-piercing bullets which achieved a fair amount
of success by putting crews out of action. Later in the
war the Germans issued to their infantry, though only
in small numbers, the first anti-tank rifle. In the
Second World War the armour of the tank was matched
against the power of penetration of the anti-tank gun
and armour-piercing shell in a fluctuating contest for
mastery.

The ring fortresses mentioned in the account of the
strategy and tactics of the First World War are particularly interesting because so much skill and such
vast sums of money went into them and they nevertheless accomplished relatively little under the test of
war, infinitely less than field-works. One feature of the
former was a steel cupola covering a fortress gun; the
two were raised together by machinery for each shot
and then lowered again. When these equipments were
designed, however, the great siege howitzers had not

appeared, but they were built in time to put Brialmont's forts out of action in 1914. The Turkish
fortress of Erzerum is not quite a fair instance because
it had not been fully modernized and was a long way
short of its quota of guns; but it had been excellently
laid out by British and later German experts. Yet the
Russian General Yudenich, with only a trifling amount
of heavy artillery, took it in February 1916 by penetration at top speed between the forts.

It must be admitted that the tendency has been to
underrate the significance of these fortresses, designed
on a basis of pure theory, when judging them in the
light of results. Some of those on the French frontier
which hardly came into action justified themselves by
the mere fact that the Germans avoided them. On the
German side Metz was useful because it split the
French front in 1914. Liège, Namur, Maubeuge, and
Antwerp bought time for the Entente. Several of the
fortresses on the Eastern Front played important roles.
Military historians are too apt to come to the conclusion that strategy, tactics, weapons, and defences
which suffer from defects can be no good at all.
Enquiry should be directed to estimating whether the
dividend they pay is sufficient to satisfy the investment. The most severe and scientific critic of the fortress
system prior to the Second World War, Sir George
Sydenham Clarke, pressed his argument too far when
he wrote: 'The best fortification, judged by results,
has been that improvised by stress of circumstances,
unspoiled by the debasing influence of the text-book.'[2]

[2] Sydenham Clarke, *Fortifications*, pp. 49, 94.

Field fortification 'improvised by stress of circumstances' did not even check the German advance in 1914, whereas the ring fortresses did.

The objections to these were, however, heavy. They were in part financial, since the large funds voted for them would probably have been better spent on increasing the efficiency of field armies which had been, in most of the countries later engaged in the First World War, sharply rationed. On the military side the failure of the forts to withstand the latest giant howitzers has been mentioned. This was hardly the fault of Brialmont, who died an octogenarian in 1903. The fortresses, however, also immobilized considerable garrisons and masses of heavy artillery. In many cases they lacked any provision for defence by infantry, so that strong field forces were needed to assist in holding them. Debit and credit pages contain items so open to dispute that it is difficult to reach a balance. What is clear is that field fortifications played an incomparably greater part than the *places fortes* in the First World War.

The Maginot Line has been even more bitterly derided. It was of a different character, a continuous line of fortifications covering, connecting, and backing a chain of large forts, each able to protect neighbours by fire; highly mechanized, with vast underground barracks and stores for ammunition and supplies, protected by anti-tank barriers and supported by mobile infantry and artillery. Its major fault—apart from the fact that it did not cover the whole frontier-line and could be turned through Belgium—was psychological, the spirit it stood for. It was the emblem of a nation, and indeed of a command, facing war without self-confidence and desiring to wage a limited kind of half-war. This attitude was fatal when dealing with a tiger such as Hitler. Of its intrinsic military strength, however, there can be no doubt. The man who framed the plan which led to the astounding German victory of 1940—a plan of which an important feature was avoidance of direct attack on the Maginot Line—has written: 'It was obvious to any military mind that the Germans would be even less keen—or able—to assault the Maginot Line of 1939 than they had the Verdun-Toul-Nancy-Épinal fortifications of 1914.'[3]

The defeat of the field army led finally to the turning of the Maginot Line. It did not prove a failure, but the aid which it gave to the field armies was unavailing because their rout was so complete. Exposed to extremely heavy bombardment, stripped of its 'interval troops', it defied all attacks. The single major fort lost was on a flank and was the only one not covered by fire from another. The line held until after the head of the Government had sued for an armistice.[4]

In this war fortresses, apart from the Maginot Line, played only a minor part, though Stalingrad and some other cities and towns, defended as extemporized fortresses, proved very effective ones. Field fortification seemed to those who recalled the previous great war to be very little practised. This was, however, only by

[3] Manstein, *Lost Victories*, p. 98.
[4] Rowe, *The Great Wall of France*, pp. 257, 272, 273, 284, 285.

comparison, and there was in fact a great deal of entrenchment. There were new features too, minefields on an enormous scale, anti-tank defences in the form of ditches—of very little value—and belts of 'dragon's teeth'—highly effective.

Above all, the search for protection was pursued as eagerly as in the First World War, in some ways even more so. In that war shelter trenches were occasionally dug in camps, especially when German night-bombing became. for the period, heavy in 1918. It was not, however, a common practice. In the Second World War the digging of narrow slit-trenches became the rule, for one side or the other and often for both. At every halt the provision of such cover was the first task. Those who have taken part in manœuvres in Germany will recall how widespread was the practice, which proved that it had been accepted as military doctrine and gave reality to mimic warfare.

Another aspect of the quest for protection was concealment. In its simplest forms it is of course extremely ancient, but in the First World War the aeroplane exposed much that had in earlier times been hidden from the man on the ground, even from the man in the basket of an observation balloon. More subtle methods of concealment were called for. They were accorded the dignity of a new word, camouflage, from the French verb *camoufler*, to disguise. The main object was to deceive the camera, but in the First World War much more often to avoid shell fire than bombs from the air. By 1 January 1916 a camouflage service was established in the British Army and the manufacture of material was organized. Some of the devices were paltry, but a great deal of the work done by British, French, German, Italian, and Austrian experts was effective.

The commonest material was netting to which tufts of material, generally green and brown on the Western Front, were affixed. Their effect was to efface not only objects below but particularly tell-tale shadows. Netting was almost invariably spread over batteries or dispersed single guns, but also over huts, sometimes in a single sheet over a small camp. At sea warships were painted in what were known as 'dazzle' patterns. On land concrete surfaces dappled with various bright colours seemed to sink into virtual invisibility. Orders were constantly issued to avoid tracks ending abruptly, because this revealed batteries, telephone exchanges, command posts and the like, which might not otherwise have been discovered. It was easier to issue orders on the subject, however, than to find a means of carrying them out.

Indeed, it never was easy to deceive the camera or the skilled interpretation of the intelligence officers. One of these young men, coaching an artillery staff officer, would, for example, point to a hardly visible mark on a photograph and announce that this was clearly a dummy battery position and that some poor fool had given it away by trying to be too clever. Those blast marks were obviously artificial. Sometimes an elaborate concrete structure was, immediately on completion, camouflaged in masterly style and then photographed by a friendly aircraft to the complete satisfaction of the builder. In fact, the enemy had added it to his collection when it was half built. The fact that it was as good as invisible was now immaterial from the gunner's point of view. In his album it was encircled in red ink. When British air bombing on the Western Front became heavy in the early summer of 1918, Ludendorff issued orders that large troop movements should be carried out at night; small huts widely dispersed should be used in new camps; camouflage must always be put up before work began; it must always be as low as possible to avoid long shadows; and care must be taken to avoid new tracks from camouflaged constructions.[5]

Camouflage was used for deception as well as concealment, as the remark about the dummy battery bears witness. It was combined with other ruses. When Allenby was preparing his final offensive against the Turks in Palestine he massed infantry and cavalry on the coast, hiding the horses in the orange groves. He was anxious that the enemy should believe he intended to attack in the Judaean hills. He therefore made mock preparations to establish G.H.Q. in Jerusalem, filled the former cavalry camps near by with dummy horses, and for good measure had the programme of a race meeting printed, the date being that on which the offensive was in fact to be launched. This was a combination of three ruses with camouflage. In the Second World War dummy tanks served the same purpose as Allenby's dummy horses.

Leaving aside the 'brazen chariots' of the ancients,

[5] Falls, *The First World War*.

armoured cars were used at the very start of the First World War. They proved valuable against the Senussi in Egypt, but the fast light tank usurped many of their functions in the Second World War. There, one of the main problems of tank design was to increase the protection afforded by armour while decreasing speed to the smallest possible extent. The Germans introduced during the war, in 1942 a 56-tonner (Tiger I) with armour of 100-mm. at its maximum and in 1944 a 68·7-tonner (Tiger II) with maximum armour of 185 mm. Both were armed with a tank version of the 88-mm. anti-aircraft gun, previously used with devastating effect as an anti-tank gun.[6] They were chiefly valuable in defence and their mobility was lessened because many bridges would not carry them. On the defensive, however, they proved deadly, especially in country with cover which permitted them to lie in wait for their prey. Though their most brilliant victories had been won with medium and even light tanks, the Germans opted for weight, even taking for granted that weight inevitably went up all round. The Panther of 1943 was regarded as a medium tank for service in the Panzer divisions, yet it weighed 44·8 tons, had armour 110-mm. thick at the maximum, and was armed with a long 75-mm. gun. The heaviest British tank, the Churchill VII, built as an infantry tank but proving versatile, weighed 40 tons with maximum armour of 152-mm. The biggest tank of the war was the Russian Stalin, mounting a 122-mm. gun.

It was not in tanks alone that armour extended its

[6] Hart, *The Tanks*, Vol. ii, p. 496.

role in the Second World War. Armoured troop carriers were used, though not until near the end, to move infantry over ground exposed to heavy fire. Armoured supply vehicles, advocated a generation earlier by the tank pioneers, were never seriously exploited.

The strengthening of armour in warships continued. The British battleships of the famous *King George V* class, all five completed after the outbreak of the Second World War, were belted with armour of 15 and 14 inches, and their turrets and barbettes were protected by 16-inch armour. Thus in about eighty years the thickness of armour had been quadrupled. Yet speed was still sought after. The Germans, with large-scale commerce raiding in view and realizing the value for this purpose of ships which could take on anything short of a modern battleship and show it a clean pair of heels, produced the *Scharnhorst* and *Gneisenau*. Armed with nine 11-inch guns, with 13-inch armour as a belt and over the turrets, they yet had a speed of 32 knots, five knots more than the maximum of the *Von der Tann* at Jutland.[7] For their purpose these were good ships. The American battleships of the *North Carolina*, *South Dakota*, and *Iowa* classes, on which the work of design began in 1935, contrived to combine excellent speed and good steering with good torpedo protection, strengthened armoured decks for protection from bombing, and 16-inch main batteries.[8] The two giants

[7] Parkes, *British Battleships*, pp. 663, 671.
[8] Commodore Dudley Wright Knox in Morison, *The Battle of the Atlantic*, p. lvi.

of the war, the Japanese *Yamato* and *Mushashi*, which mounted 18-inch guns, had no luck. The two most powerful battleships ever built were doomed to fight in a war in which the role of the battleship had lessened and in an ocean where the role fell below the average. They were not actively engaged in the earlier operations in which battleships were involved because they were not needed. They perished without having given an adequate return for all the money, toil, and skill that had gone into them. Their sole contribution was a measure of respect and caution imposed on American admirals when these monsters were or might be in the neighbourhood.

The earliest aircraft had been too light and flimsy to carry any form of armour. This situation had, however, changed greatly by the opening of the Second World War, though the 'stick and string' type biplanes survived until within only about two years from it. The most notable example of the importance of armour in aircraft was provided in the struggle between American and Japanese forces. The Japanese gained many brilliant successes in the early stages of the war with their fast and generally long-ranged aircraft flown by highly trained pilots and crews. The lack of armour relatively to the Americans proved, however, a terrible handicap. In the latter part of the war it led to a fantastic disparity in casualties. In the Battle of the Philippine Sea of 19 June 1944, the biggest carrier battle of the war and popularly remembered in the United States as 'the great Marianas Turkey Shoot', the Japanese lost about 315 aircraft including about

50 land-based, to an American loss of 29.[9] This extraordinary result was to a considerable extent due to the skill, intelligence, and courage of the American airmen, but the main factor was without doubt the lack of protection of the Japanese aircraft. The Japanese Admiral rightly fought the action of 19 June at the extreme effective range of his aircraft, which was slightly greater than those of the American Admiral Mitscher, so that on this day—though not in the action of 20 June, the results of which have not been considered here—the Japanese were on the offensive throughout. Yet the damage inflicted on the American fleet was trifling.

This was also the first war in which civil defence, including methods of protection, played a big part. In the First World War 'cellar life' had been a feature of the adversities of Paris, which actually came under the fire of specially built long-range guns in 1918, as well as aircraft bombing. In the East End of London air raids caused a tendency to panic in the latter part of 1917, and, whether there was a raid or not, some 300,000 people crowded each night into the underground railway stations and slept on the platforms.[10] Zeppelins and the bombing aeroplanes known as Gothas were, however, only a warning of what was to come. There was little organized civil defence beyond the reduction of lights.

In the Second World War a ministry was formed for the task. Shelters were issued to householders who

[9] Morison, *New Guinea and the Marianas*, p. 277.
[10] Jones, *The War in the Air*, Vol. V, p. 89.

had space enough for them. Hundreds of thousands of basements were strengthened with beams and supports. Many who could afford the cost built themselves deep shelters, roofed with concrete and lit by electricity, in gardens or even the areas of town houses. (Some in London areas remained in existence a dozen years after the war because, unless with the aid of dynamite, it seemed almost impossible to demolish them.) Fire services were reinforced by whole-time personnel, with engines generally lighter than those of the fire brigades but modern and efficient. Bodies of wardens, fire-watchers, rescue workers, and others were formed. Germany, subjected to the heaviest bombing, organized the strongest defences, including a number of vast concrete structures, mass shelters. Needless to say, sleeping on the platforms of underground railways was repeated. Evacuation from vulnerable cities and towns took place on an enormous scale, organized by governments or carried out by individuals on their own initiative. People who continued to work in cities often slept outside them.

In some cases the civil side of the quest for protection exercised a strong effect upon warfare in the field. Thus, the Germans dispersed factories and workshops widely as a counter to air bombing. This measure was strikingly successful in maintaining production of war material, but in the last stage developed a fatal disadvantage. When the whole system of communications was dislocated by British and American bombing the material could not be shifted for assembling, except in a trickle. That which was assembled was yet more difficult to deliver to the troops engaged with the Russians to the east and Eisenhower's allied forces to the west.

The battle between the missile and means of protection against it has thus been continuous, 'from the earliest times to the present day'. The missile has generally been the stronger, though not to as great an extent as might be supposed at first glance. It is true that a good missile weapon has in the majority of cases, though by no means always, been capable of piercing the protection against which it is directed. A direct hit, or at all events a near miss is, however, required. On 1 July 1916, when the first assault of the Battle of the Somme was launched, the German defenders in deep dug-outs excavated in the chalk, with a handful of watchers on the stairs, had not been put out of action on the greater part of the front, and the result is only too well remembered. In the Second World War units in hastily dug slit-trenches were subjected to heavy bombardments which frequently inflicted little loss, in some cases none. In cities bombed from the air shelters and cellars saved thousands of lives. Even dining-room tables occasionally preserved from death people whose houses were largely demolished. It was always bad policy, certainly until 1945, to be defeatist about the value of means of protection against the most powerful weapons.

How far does this remain true? In the year mentioned we entered a new era, that of weapons of hitherto inconceivable power and horror. Many who then concluded that the ultimate force of destruction had been reached have watched the development of enormously greater power. The majority have concluded that, at best, the only defence is retention of the ability to retaliate. Nuclear war must be considered separately. Here all that need be said is that a number of governments have not even now abandoned the quest for protection. Were the steps they have taken for military protection as well known as their work in civil defence this endeavour would appear far more striking than it does to the mass of the people.

Chapter Seven

SEA WARFARE IN THE AGE OF
STEAM

THE introduction of steam propulsion in warships was a slow process, beset by doubts and hesitations. It increased the risk of fire without at first producing greater speed. Paddle-boxes impaired sailing qualities and were also vulnerable to gunfire, as were engines and boilers.[1] In this respect the introduction of the screw marked a step forward because engines could be set lower, well below the water line. The handicap of decreased range persisted because steamers had to coal frequently, whereas sailing ships could keep the seas for six months, stocked with all that was needed for men and guns except fresh water. The first screw-propelled steamer was launched in 1832, but the first really efficient screw-propelled battleship may be said to have been the French *Gloire*, launched in 1859—though efficiency must be measured to a great extent by what the other fellow has got. The *Gloire* started a ship-building race between France and Britain.

Parallel with the shift from sail to steam was the improvement of the gun and its projectile. Naval guns firing horizontal shells were tested in France as early as 1824, but again the advance was slow. At first shell-firing guns had to be served in the same way as Nelson's

[1] Baxter, *The Introduction of the Ironclad Warship*, p. 11.

because they were muzzle-loaders. Loading at the breech came in just over half-way through the nineteenth century and in the same period armour, the direct reply to the shell-firing gun, challenged it sharply. Ship-designers produced the gun-turret; gun-designers strengthened guns to stand higher charges. The ceaseless war between gun and armour had commenced.

Meanwhile steam had deeply influenced naval strategy and tactics. It rendered ships independent of the wind. It afforded a wider choice in the use of harbours. Henceforth it was no longer desirable to avoid a fleet anchorage facing the prevailing wind or one far to leeward of that from which a hostile fleet would operate, as in the day of Admiral Lord St. Vincent.[2] On the other hand, naval bases became more important than ever. An ocean-going fleet depended on coaling-stations, and, though it might have colliers available, it could seldom coal at sea. A wretched little place like Aden became a vital asset.

Tactically, much of the skill in seamanship which had won for Britain so many battles became, if one dare say so, redundant. The tactics of sail were closely connected with the direction and strength of the wind and sometimes with skilled prognostications of changes which might occur. The manœuvring before battle was intricate and often brilliant. Manœuvre remained essential under steam and in some cases might depend on the weather, to the extent, for example, of obtaining the windward station in order to give the enemy the smoke; but the niceties were gone.

[2] Falls, *A Hundred Years of War*, p. 100.

As late as the Battle of Lissa in 1866 both sides, Austrians and Italians, had actually many more wooden ships than ironclads, but that was only because time, and perhaps money, had not sufficed for a complete conversion. The future was clear. The doom of the wooden warship was signed. Warships would be built of iron or steel, propelled by screws, with armoured sides and iron decks and mounting breech-loading rifled guns.[3]

The nineteenth century, after the year 1815, witnessed relatively few great wars, though a multitude of small ones, and in the greatest, the Franco-Prussian War, the naval factor was of infinitesimal importance. In the Crimean War naval power was decisive because the British and French allies could not have entered the Black Sea, much less captured Sevastopol, without the ability to dominate the Russian fleet. In fact, Russia was subjected to a heavier strain in maintaining land communications with the Crimea than Britain and France in maintaining sea communications. The one naval battle, Sinope, fought on 30 November 1853, rammed home the lesson already accepted. The ships on both sides were wooden, but the Russians possessed shell-firing guns, and the Turks did not. The Turkish squadron was annihilated in a couple of hours.

The American Civil War included small battles fought for the most part to enter or defend inlets of the sea or navigable rivers of strategic value. The outstanding feature, however, was the Federal blockade

[3] Falls, *A Hundred Years of War*, p. 102. And see p. 61, above.

and Confederate efforts to break it. It was to a great extent a war of improvisation, even for the more highly industrialized North. For instance, in the capture of New Orleans Farragut hung chain cables outside his hulls and stacked sand-bags round his engines as makeshift armour. In the war of 1866 the Austrians won the Battle of Lissa with a fleet inferior to the Italian but a brilliant Admiral, Freiherr von Tegetthoff.

By the opening of the twentieth century battleships mounted 12-in. guns and were generally protected by belts of thick armour on the water line and thinner plating higher up. A new naval power was revealed when Japan went to war with Russia in 1904. Though she had not as yet launched an armoured warship and had had to depend on foreign yards, her naval leaders, above all her great Commander-in-Chief Admiral Togo, knew their business thoroughly. The Battle of the Yellow Sea has been accounted the first great naval engagement of 'modern times', but much has happened since these words were applied to it. It was followed over eight months later, on 27 May 1905, by the Tsushima, in which the Russian Baltic Fleet, after a voyage half-way round the world, was met by Togo and virtually destroyed. Again sea power was all-important. The Japanese fleet provided the conditions under which the army struck decisive blows. In the course of the war one Russian and two Japanese battleships were sunk by mines.

The First World War confirmed the importance of sea power, that is, adequate though not necessarily complete control of the main oceanic routes. In other ways it left expectations unfulfilled. The war had been preceded by a race in naval ship-building and armaments between Britain and Germany, but in four years and a quarter only one great 'battleship battle'— Jutland—was fought, and it was indecisive. The truth was that the weaker side, the German, could not hope to fight with a prospect of success unless with the aid of luck in reducing the British Grand Fleet by torpedoes and mines, and that the successive British Commanders-in-Chief became haunted by the fear of disaster at the hands of submarines. The war at sea developed into a war of British blockade and German counter-offensive, mainly with submarines. It was a new chapter in the old story of keeping open trade routes and denying them to the enemy.

The chief feature of the blockade was simple: mercantile blockade to drive the enemy's merchantmen off the seas and to capture or destroy those which attempted to continue their tasks. Allied with this was the naval blockade, the laying of defensive minefields to block straits and harbour entrances, and what may be called offensive mining, to make dangerous certain areas in the open sea which hostile fleets had an inducement to cross.[4] This was accompanied by rationing imports to neutrals based on statistics of pre-war imports. The first and most important part of the programme, the mercantile blockade, was overwhelmingly successful.

The German submarine, distressing though it was,

[4] Domville-Fife, *Submarines and Sea Power*, pp. 212–15.

presented no serious problem until the introduction of the 'unrestricted' campaign, the sinking of ships, neutrals included, without warning or possibility of rescuing crews. The sinkings rose to a terrible height, 169 British ships alone being sunk in April 1917. 'The continuance of this rate of loss would have brought disaster upon all the allied campaigns and might well have involved an unconditional surrender.'[5] The main counter-measure, the introduction of convoy, brought about a drop in the graph of losses almost as steep as the rise. From June 1917 the losses of German submarines increased sharply, and in 1918 the growth of British and American ship-building helped to assure the final triumph over the U-boats. It had been a near-run thing, however. It is notable that from late 1914 'marine' losses, that is from normal marine risks, were always, where Britain was concerned, higher than losses suffered from German raiders, cruisers, and mines. These marine losses were in large part from collisions due to sailing without lights in convoy. But in that period almost all losses, except through submarines, were negligible.[6]

The opportunities of British submarines and those of Britain's allies were for obvious reasons very limited by comparison. They none the less struck some heavy blows. They could penetrate into the Baltic and the Sea of Marmara, which no allied surface warship could enter, and they made their presence felt in both. On both sides submarines exercised an important influence

[5] Salter, *Allied Shipping Control*, p. 122.
[6] Ibid., p. 131.

on the minds of the opposing commanders. The torpedo became a deadly weapon, but at its deadliest when carried by a submarine and used against merchantmen. In destroyers it was curiously ineffective at Jutland.

That battle provided food for the mind. The British dreadnoughts were probably superior to the German, but only four were heavily engaged and the majority did not fire a salvo. The battle emphasized the value of quick thinking, design, and high-quality guns and shell as clearly as that of gunnery. These features were found in the German Admiral Hipper and his battle-cruiser squadron. He led his force with skill and daring. The ships withstood heavy pounding and only one of the four was lost. Yet they were also fast. One of the earlier battle cruisers, the *Von der Tann*, exceeded 27 knots at Jutland. The *Derfflinger*, begun in 1911 and armed with 12-in. guns as against the *Von der Tann's* 11-in., must be accounted the best ship, and the best shooting ship, of the type. Britain had kept a jump ahead in the calibre of guns but at the expense of protection,[7] and that flaw, combined with good German guns and shells and gunnery—in several cases extremely close salvoes—resulted in the loss of three battle cruisers. In another respect the High Seas Fleet was strong for a young navy: Grand Admiral von Tirpitz, its founder, attributed vast importance to fire-fighting, and crews were worked up to high skill in it. The *Seydlitz* was at one time in flames and almost hidden by masses of black smoke extending into the heavens, but she

[7] Parkes, *British Battleships*, pp. 308, 343.

reached port and was ready to go to sea again within four months.

To some extent this war followed the pattern which had become familiar. Britain provided by far the most powerful naval contingent in a coalition the majority of whose members were also naval powers. Owing to her strength these allies were enabled to use all the open seas as they would. With the aid of the United States Navy, that country, after the military disasters on the Western Front in the first half of 1918, transported to France more than twice the number of troops originally considered necessary. The blockade which was established and maintained became an important factor in the defeat of the Central Powers, though German historians have exaggerated its effects in order to relieve the Army of the odium of that disaster. And victory in the submarine war was practically assured long before it was established in the land war and without any sensible aid from operations on land. It was in a sense an echo of old wars in which the French, their regular fleets having been defeated, reverted to *la guerre de course*, attack on British ocean trade by privateers, won great successes and caused heavy losses, but failed in the end because they could not defeat the main fleet or fleets in the hands of which the final verdict rested.

At the same time, the First World War exposed the weaknesses of sea power. Blockade may be an instrument of strangulation, but that is a slow process when the enemy has at his disposal or can conquer the resources of a fruitful continent. Napoleon was defeated rather through his military disaster in Russia than by the direct effects of blockade, though it was the need to stop leakages in his continental system that induced him to undertake the Russian campaign. The conquest of Rumania in 1916 and of the Ukraine in 1917 and 1918 proved telling counter-strokes to naval blockade because these two regions contained vast and rich farmlands. Then railways, which in the most highly civilized and industrialized countries had reached their highest development by 1914, robbed sea power of certain of its advantages and removed some of the anxieties with which it had earlier been regarded by belligerents facing navies stronger than their own. Germany and Austria-Hungary had never lost sight of the needs of war in laying lines. The Germans could always move troops between France and other European theatres of war far more speedily by rail than Britain and France could move them by water, and even where France had railway connexions with an ally, Italy, their capacity was inferior to those of Germany and Austria combined. The overthrow of Serbia in 1915 was as much a riposte to the efforts of sea power as the occupation of the Ukraine. It was carried out chiefly for the purpose of reopening the main line to Constantinople so that Turkey should not run short of material, especially shell, to defend the Gallipoli Peninsula.

The Second World War began with no navies comparable in strength to the British Grand Fleet and the German High Seas Fleet of the First. This state of affairs was due in part to international agreements which exercised an influence even after they had come to an end; in part to Hitler's lack of interest in sea power; and to some extent to the greatly increased cost of naval ship-building. A transformation had been brought about by the advance of aircraft as an instrument in naval war, and within the span of the conflict they greatly increased in range and power. The aircraft carrier became the type on which decisions most often hinged, especially in the Pacific, where all the greatest naval battles were fought. Italy, with a considerable fleet, had built no carriers, in the erroneous belief that in Mediterranean waters shore-based aircraft could provide her fleet with adequate air support in all circumstances. Germany had none either, and France was, as a nation, driven out of the war at an early stage, with the consequence that the great bulk of her navy was laid up, disarmed, or scuttled.

The three nations which provide material for an estimation of the role of carriers are therefore the United States, the United Kingdom, and Japan. It was Japanese naval officers who started with the clearest conception of the role of the carrier and who realized that a battle fleet strong in this type of ship and in aircraft would dominate one composed mainly of battleships. They were beaten largely owing to the enormously superior industrial efficiency of their foe and their inability to develop their fighter, bomber, and torpedo-carrying aircraft as fast as the United States. Their carriers did not fail them. Their aircraft did, and this failure led to enormous losses in crews with which their training capacity could not compete.

If steam had partly divested naval tactics of their subtle seamanship, the carriers restored it. In launching and taking in its aircraft the carrier had to turn into the wind, so that a pursuit to leeward was very slow. The choice of the right moment to fly off aircraft; the decision as to whether bombers, torpedoplanes or fighters should have priority on the flight deck; and (when more than one carrier was available) the decision as to whether or not to hold on to a reserve —on such factors might hang the balance between victory and defeat.

The torpedo was the carrier's deadliest weapon. Since it was also the main weapon of the destroyer and the submarine it must be considered the outstanding naval weapon of the war. In the submarine it maintained the power displayed in the First World War and in the destroyer surpassed it; in the battle fleet it stole the dominant role from the big gun.

Another feature was the development of radar, which expanded till, late in the contest, fire could be directed by it against unseen targets. The long lead in radar maintained by the Americans over the Japanese was a vital factor in victory. And yet science did not completely eclipse the role of the humble individual seaman. In the Battle of Savo Island (off Guadalcanal) fought on 9 August 1942, the Japanese possessed no radar equipment, whereas the American-Australian fleet mounted some, though admittedly of an early type. The astonishing Japanese success in 'one of the worst defeats ever inflicted on the United States

Navy',[8] was largely due to Japanese eyesight in a night attack. This is coming down to bedrock.

In the Mediterranean British carriers played a fine part against the Italians. Here, however, conditions were utterly different from those of the Pacific and far more dangerous for these ships. Risks from land-based bombers, hardly appreciable in the vast ocean, were grave in the narrow inland sea, especially in or near the Sicilian Narrows. In these circumstances the attack on the Italian fleet in Taranto Harbour on the night of 11 November 1940 with the relatively small force of twenty torpedo aircraft was as bold as it was successful. Three battleships, one of them of the most modern type, were sunk, though in shallow water. The result was that British convoys were undisturbed for some six weeks, and though this proved a gleam of false daylight, it was useful. The other battle exploit was that of Cape Matapan, when three Italian heavy cruisers were sunk during the night of 28–29 March 1941 after another modern Italian battleship had been seriously damaged by a torpedo aircraft. Thereafter the Royal Navy's work in the Mediterranean was in the main that of covering convoys, attempting to interrupt Italian and German communications with North Africa, and playing its part in combined operations.

These were a striking feature of the Second World War by comparison with the First, in which the attack on the Gallipoli Peninsula had been the only notable example. Sea power not only rendered these

[6] Morison, *The Struggle for Guadalcanal*, p. 17.

possible but in certain cases sustained the landing forces when in trouble. At Salerno in September 1943 five escort carriers, in their turn protected by aircraft from two big carriers, supplemented the very limited support which could be given by land-based aircraft from Sicilian airfields, and four battleships made an immense contribution to the break-up of the German counter-offensive.[9] After the landing in Normandy on 6 June, 1944 the process was repeated. In the Pacific naval fire often provided the sole artillery support in the capture of islands of strategic value.

The submarine war was reproduced in the later world war but in vastly different circumstances. In the First World War, valuable as was the achievement of British submarines, Britain and her allies were almost entirely on the defensive in this feature of the conflict. In the Second World War American submarines not only accounted for nearly 30 per cent. of all Japanese warships sunk, but proved the deadliest killer of Japanese freighters. They sank about 60 per cent. of the gross tonnage of tankers destroyed.

It must be a matter of opinion whether the new U-boat threat was the more serious. In our study of the art of war the main task is to outline the differences. The U-boat was in itself more formidable. Its range and speed were greater, and the use of very large boats, known popularly as 'milch cows', to refuel the fighting boats at sea afforded them greater scope. The increased range of aircraft was a factor both in attack and defence, but on balance favoured the latter. With the aid of

[9] Falls, *A Hundred Years of War*, p. 347.

radar British aircraft were before the end of 1941 beginning to attack U-boats by night as well as day. British listening gear became far superior to that of the First World War. In 1944 the Germans introduced the *Schnorkel*, a pipe admitting enough air from the surface to keep Diesel engines running. The layman would conclude that this was a sure battle-winner, since the U-boat fitted with it could remain continuously submerged and to a large extent nullify the aircraft, by now its deadliest foe. The *Schnorkel* was indeed an asset. In fact, however, the results were not impressive. Most of the U-boats' success had been gained by their high surface speed, which had brought them within sight of victory in 1942. They became less effective against convoys and their concentration of attacks in inshore British waters proved disappointing.[10]

The availability of bases for submarines, the destroyers which fought them, and still more the aircraft which both opposed and supported them played a great part. With the conquest of France Germany was able to extend her base-line from the North Cape to the Pyrenees. Britain was hampered by the loss of First World War bases in now neutral Southern Ireland, though Ulster proved an invaluable air outpost and convoy escort terminal. On the other hand, the anti-submarine war was, after the United States had become a belligerent, waged from both sides of the Atlantic simultaneously, which represented an enormous increase in the strength of the opposition. A lesser but still valuable one was Portuguese permission to

[10] Creswell, *Sea Warfare 1939–1945*, p. 243.

make use of airfields in the Azores. From them long-range aircraft could close the dangerous gap in mid-Atlantic between those operating from British bases in the east and American in the west.

The famous German method of attack by 'wolf packs' involved movement on the surface for the sake of speed because the units did not actually hunt in a pack but formed one when a report from a single submarine was picked up by the control in France. At the height of its success this was a terrible method of destruction. Between August and November 1942 some strongly-escorted convoys lost nearly half their ships, and 2,000,000 tons of shipping were sunk in these four months. The decisive defeat of the U-boats, despite the final effort in the *Schnorkel* phase, came in May 1943. In that month they lost forty-one boats, about one-third of all at sea. To this victory the R.A.F. Coastal Command, which included all shore-based aircraft in Britain taking part in anti-submarine warfare, made a great contribution.

The instruments of sea power and through them the art of war at sea changed vastly from one war to the other. By the end of the Second the battleship was on its way out. It was for some time believed that the carrier would go the same way, but presently there began a heavy programme of carrier building, especially in the United States. The role of the carrier and carrier-borne aircraft with nuclear weapons must depend on its prospects of survival against a great hostile offensive with the same weapons. This is matter for speculation, but in 'conventional' wars the carrier—

not necessarily the largest—is clearly invaluable. The submarine might prove as effective in a short war as it did in two long ones. Sea power and the art of war at sea may have entered their final phase, but that phase is not likely to end for some time—nor, if an all-out war is avoided, for a long time.

Chapter Eight

TOTAL WAR

WHEN the phrase 'total war' was first used the harnessing of atomic energy had not been carried out and only a minute body of scientists had any conception of how this was to be done. The concept of totality is thus independent of atomic or nuclear warfare. Some of those who first encountered the phrase became intoxicated by its significance, grim though it was, and talked nonsense about it. If we look at the history of war or even examine war in the abstract, we shall find it natural that some wars should be more, or less, limited than others. The causes, the aims of the belligerents, the prospects of outside intervention, the temper and philosophy of the times—these and other factors must influence the manner and means of waging war.

Then, the very fact that a big war has been conducted without restraint or scruple may lead to a reaction. The Thirty Years War was marked by horrible excesses and left a great part of Germany in devastation. This resulted in an effort to canalize war, powerfully influenced by the immortal work of the Dutch jurist Hugo Grotius, who died in 1645, three years before the war dragged its way to an end. He built up a system of jurisprudence to distinguish between just wars and those brought on by ambition and greed for conquest. He took this line because he believed that it was waste of time to try to eliminate war altogether. In the same spirit he advocated the observance of moral obligations such as respect for neutrality and humanity to women and children. *The Rights of War and Peace*, together with some successors of lesser merit and the memory of rulers and statesmen, played a part in the relative humanity and restraint in the waging of war throughout the remainder of the seventeenth century and the greater part of the next. When these virtues were laid aside, as in the two ravagings of the Palatinate by order of Louis XIV, measures which had been commonplace in the Thirty Years War were found shocking by many.

'Just as limitation can never be absolute, so also totality in war is a relative concept rather than an absolute one.'[1] Total war in the absolute would involve fighting without any restrictions, even those of prudence and self-interest. This did not happen. For example, it has often been asserted that the wars sparked off by the Reformation, the 'Wars of Religion', approached totality. They were assuredly unrestrained, 'unselective' in their aims, and generally barbarous. Yet when Queen Elizabeth intervened in 1585 in the struggle of the Dutch against the Spaniards she did not declare war, any more than did Philip II. She professed a desire to see all the subjects of the King of Spain in the Low Countries living in a state of 'due obedience' to him; she engaged from time to time in peace negotiations; and on the

[1] Preston, Wise, and Werner, *Men in Arms*, p. 15.

Dutch side merchants revictualled the Spaniards by sea.[2]

This is by no means to deny that war has become closer to totality in modern times, since the French Revolution. In earlier chapters an effort has been made to show that the determination of the rulers of revolutionary France to fight a people's war and the response they received initiated the change. Napoleon exploited the virtues of the young armies of the Revolution by his genius. It has also been indicated that railways gave the process a push forward, and that here the prime exploiters were generals of the American Civil War and the elder Moltke. The final impetus was given by the combined progress of science and industry.

The technique of fighting a blockade can justly be considered as part of the art of war. Napoleon showed how clearly he understood the problems of a war not unlimited indeed but approaching in its economic aspect closer to totality than any international conflict of the past. He became the pioneer of the beet-sugar industry because the blockade cut off cane sugar from France. This was only one of his achievements in the stimulation of agriculture, the yield of which increased roughly five-fold during his rule. In eight years the number of silk-looms in France increased threefold. He was the originator of the woollen industry of Roubaix. He set up factories for the machine-printing of fabrics and especially the imitation of Indian cashmeres, which could no longer be imported.[3] It has

[2] Falls, *Mountjoy, Elizabethan General*. p. 30.
[3] Falls, *Ordeal by Battle*, p. 50.

been said of him that he was to be seen leaning over the customs statements as he did over his reports when on campaign.

The industrial revolution, originating in England, is considered by some to have got into its stride a few years before Napoleon's birth in 1769. In certain respects—for example, the development of iron-smelting by coke—it affected his wars materially, but it did not appear as a decisive factor until the middle of the nineteenth century. How small, or at all events, how uneven, was the psychological impact of the life-and-death struggle with Napoleon is witnessed by the many cases in which this is disregarded in the literature of the period. Sprigs of the nobility and the wealthier squire-archy, whose descendants have in more recent times been the most eager to serve in war, often, like so many of the writers, disregarded the Napoleonic Wars. Fox-hunting was passing through a brilliant phase. George Osbaldeston, the almost legendary hard rider and M.F.H., does not mention Napoleon or Wellington in his memoirs. One passage runs: 'We had the most extraordinary sport during my period of office in the Burton country (1810–1813). The gentlemen of the hunt presented me with a large silver waiter having foxes' heads as handles, with a most complimentary inscription on the back, as a token of their appreciation.'[4] In 1810 'Squire' Osbaldeston reached the age of twenty-four. Few signs appear of contempt on the part of the country at large or even of officers of their own class for those who lived such lives.

[4] Cuming, *Squire Osbaldeston*, p. 17.

The features of the mid-nineteenth century affecting the form and conduct of war have already been mentioned. They are the power of steam, the more fruitful cultivation of the earth, the increased extent and speed of industrial production, and the closely allied growth of populations. These contributed to a nearer approach to total war, in the sense of involving a far greater proportion of the nation and the national effort. Even now, however, inconsistencies and lacunae are to be found. The American Civil War was unlimited and approached totality in some respects. Both sides put forth tremendous efforts measured in man-power and production. Sherman deliberately destroyed the Confederacy's very means of existence. On the other hand, government controls were of the slightest. Large quantities of boots were held in Virginia at a time when the Confederate armies were nearly barefoot. States' rights were sacred to the Confederacy and Jefferson Davis would not infringe them even in such an emergency. His attitude here is completely opposed to the principle of totality. Governments which adopt this principle are as insistent in their demands on their own citizens as they are ruthless in their conduct of the war against their enemies.

The Franco-Prussian War was in some ways a signpost to totality rather than an example of it. The demands by the opposing States upon their man-power were heavy, but not on the scale of the twentieth century. The French at the time protested bitterly against Prussian reprisals for the acts of *francs-tireurs*, but many jurists have since held that the retaliation was not in general contrary to the laws of war. In the siege of Paris the Germans showed restraint. Such bombardments of the city as took place were light and for the most part brief, obviously intended as a warning rather than to cause widespread destruction. The German command has been condemned for forcing prominent Frenchmen to travel on railway engines in order to prevent the wrecking of trains. Even here the greatest English authority on the laws and usages of war, Professor L. Oppenheim, found it difficult to agree with the majority opinion that this practice was indefensible.

How steep has been the descent from the generally accepted standards of the mid-nineteenth century may be measured by two quotations. At the outset of the war of 1848 between Austria and Sardinia, when Milan rose against the garrison, Field-Marshal Radetzky decided to abandon the city. He was supremely confident that he would return victoriously, as in fact he did in the following year; but he took this grave step largely to save Milan from destruction and despite the often inhuman killing of his men in isolated posts. He said himself: 'What would Europe have to say, even though we are assailed in our most sacred rights, wounded in our innermost hearts, if we should degrade ourselves to the level of Vandals?'[5]

The second is from the book of a senior French officer, General Derrécagaix, writing some twenty years after the Franco-Prussian war, in which he had taken part: 'There exists, in a word, a law of war generally

[5] Regele, *Feldmarschall Radetzky*, p. 267.

regarded as being in force, which forbids the destruction of the enemy because that is an act of barbarism; which condemns vengeance because it is odious; which teaches nations to limit wars to reparation for an injury or the guarantee of a pledge; which forbids the infliction of useless sufferings . . . which condemns burning and devastation. . . . The conqueror ought to be generous; prisoners are brothers in arms whom the lot of conflict has betrayed; they should not be subject to any but good treatment. Goods should never become booty. Pillage is no longer permitted, not even as a reprisal.'[6]

He was writing of ideals which he knew were not and would not always be observed, but so is an author who discusses business integrity. He was writing of standards widely accepted. What were the standards of half a century later? In the Second World War fleets of aircraft on both sides set out loaded with bombs for the purpose of devastation and incendiaries for the purpose of burning. And their targets were not as a rule their foes in arms and uniform but the civil populations of cities, including the women and children. Towns were pulverized by bombs because troops lacked the leadership to take them by manœuvre, sometimes when in fact they were not occupied by hostile troops. The mass slaughter ordered by Hitler, Stalin's deliberate and cold-blooded shooting of a large proportion of the Polish officers in his hands and the most distinguished civilians in all walks of life, were revivals of practices which could not be paralleled for

[6] Derrécagaix, *La Guerre Moderne*, Vol. i, p. 23.

centuries in the annals of warfare between civilized nations.

These last were the savageries of inhumanly savage men. It must not be concluded that all those who permitted and organized the measures of warfare were barbarous by nature. They fought with the weapons which science and industry had put into their hands. Some, even of the most senior air force commanders, had qualms about the policy, notably the Americans, General Henry H. Arnold, Commanding General Army Air Forces, and General Carl Spaatz, Commanding General U.S. Army Air Forces in Europe. 'All proposals frankly aimed at breaking the morale of the German people met the consistent opposition of General Spaatz, who repeatedly raised the moral issue involved.'[7] How shameful that here American sentiment was humanitarian, and British barbarian! It is beside the point that Spaatz did not protest against 'terror' bombing by the British allies of the United States but against being drawn into it himself, and that the Americans had an aircraft suitable for bombing by daylight, whereas the British had not, so that they could only bomb indiscriminately or not at all.

At the moment these words are written the national Red Cross Societies are celebrating the centenary of the Battle of Solferino in 1859 because it was here that the Swiss Henri Dunant, appalled by the break-down of the medical services and the sufferings of the wounded, first conceived the idea of an international organization to canalize war and mitigate its horrors.

[7] *Army Air Forces in World War II*, Vol. iii, p. 638.

The celebrations of the International Committee of the Red Cross, which has its seat at Geneva, await the centenary of its actual foundation in 1864. The occasion may be one to justify pride in magnificent work achieved, but it has a melancholy and deeply alarming side. It is the International Red Cross which has from the first worked out schemes to humanize war, to purge it of needless cruelty, to protect civilians and above all women and children, and has presented to Governments detailed and practical schemes, which it has then invited them to sign. The first half-century was heartening; the second has been disappointing. Disregard of their undertakings has been widespread on the part of the most highly civilized states. Unwillingness to undertake fresh obligations has been equally general. When conferences of experts meet to lay the foundations of new conventions, international lawyers, especially those who represent or are citizens of the great powers—men of the highest integrity and the purest philanthropy—intervene to point out that such and such a proposal to protect at least a proportion of those endangered by the abominable weapons is not worth putting forward because it is wholly impracticable. The International Committee can maintain its noble work in relief of suffering as the result of war, in its inspections of the quarters of prisoners of war and concentration camps, where its recommendations are generally carried out. In its greater-scale tasks it is subject to unceasing frustration.

Yet, let it be repeated, governments have seldom acted with conscious brutality, unless when in the hands of savage autocrats such as Hitler and Stalin. They have been borne along upon the social, industrial, and scientific tide. A major war has now come to involve in principle one 'waged by means of all the man-power, all the energies, and all the material and moral resources of the state, and directed in "totality" against the hostile state. It is all-in warfare, nothing being held back by the state which practices it and no objective being avoided, so long as attack upon it may damage the enemy.'[8] Where it falls short in practice of this concept the reason has not been doubt of the principle's validity. It has been due to the influence of convenience or to inability to reach the standard, occasionally to the force of public opinion. Since, wholly in theory and in the Second World War nearly in practice, war is directed against nations as such, against their industries which provide the means of war as much as the men in uniform who use these means, it follows that the conception of illegitimate objectives or targets ceases to have any significance. British policy in the Second World War was to break the spirit of the German people by indiscriminate bombing, and the Air Ministry's object was 'the elimination of the Reich's fifty largest cities'.[9]

The restrictions imposed at home are a natural corollary to this state of affairs. If every hostile activity is to be the object of attack, no home activity can be allowed to go to waste. Finance and agriculture must be organized as thoroughly as industry. Private

[8] Falls, *Ordeal by Battle*, p. 14.
[9] Bryant, *The Turn of the Tide*, p. 500.

property must lose its rights. Food consumption must be rationed till it scarcely exceeds the minimum needed for subsistence and enough strength to work for the war effort. These measures are not in themselves shocking, but when in the cause of security laws which have been regarded as among the finest of our heritages are abrogated, when people languish in prison without trial and even without a charge, they become yet another threat to civilization. The bad example is too easily and too often copied in other circumstances when the excuses of danger and fear are absent. The whole system of restrictions has indeed the further disadvantage that it opens the eyes of left-wingers of the autocratic type to opportunities which would not otherwise have become available to them and which they would not otherwise even have perceived. It shows them how to get their hands on banking, industry, trade, communications, transport, the land, in fact upon the State as a whole. They are of course prepared to use a share of the spoils in special subsidies to those most likely to vote for them, for instance, those who rent houses rather than those who have saved up to buy them. This poses the prospect not merely of the Socialist State but, in the long run, of the Marxist-Communist State. A far tougher organization will find its material ready-made and in due time walk in to take possession.

The supreme examples of the methods of total war are to be found, as might be expected, in the Second World War. They are the bombing of London and Berlin, the German attack on England with the flying bomb and rocket bomb (V1 and V2), and the dropping of two atomic bombs on Hiroshima and Nagasaki. They are the supreme examples because the attacks were delivered against non-combatants and as measures of blind destruction. By comparison with the other targets London came off lightly in 1940 and 1941 only because the German Air Force was not adequately designed for strategic bombing. The long-range weapons of 1944 missed their intended effect only because their development had been interrupted by attacks on their experimental station at Peenemünde and on their launching sites, so that they had to be used too early. The lengthy bombardment of Berlin laid practically the whole city in ruins. It was the British night bombing that did most of the damage, and in this case virtually the only objective was Berlin itself. The aim was to get the bombers over the city and then shovel out the bombs as fast as possible. Great pride was expressed in the 'block-busters' because a single one of them was supposed to be capable of demolishing a whole block. The atom bombs did far more. Two bombs caused destruction such as the world had never witnessed. Here the aim was to break the will of Government and people without having to fight the Japanese Army.

The war which began on 25 June 1950 when the Communist forces of North Korea crossed the 38th parallel of latitude and invaded the southern part of the peninsula was relieved by one feature which takes us back to the limited type of warfare waged by Queen Elizabeth against the Spaniards in the Netherlands.

Communist China took over the conduct of the war after the North Korean armies had been virtually destroyed. The Chinese troops, however, were called 'volunteers'; neither the United States, which bore the main burden in the name of the United Nations, nor Britain, the next most important partner, nor any of the other countries which sent contingents, went to war with Communist China; and neither side went to extremes. Atomic weapons were not used; the United Nations did not bomb Chinese air bases north of the Yalu; China did not attack Hong Kong. So strong was determination in the United States Government to maintain the restrictions that when the United Nations Commander-in-Chief, General MacArthur, advocated their withdrawal his proposal was negatived. A few months later he was relieved of his command. He had advocated four steps: a blockade of China, the destruction by naval gunfire and air bombing of China's industrial capacity to wage war, the reinforcement of the United Nations army in Korea by troops of the Nationalist Army in Formosa, and the abandonment of restrictions against the employment of these troops on the Chinese mainland. If we suppose the circumstances—and the weapons—to be carried back a generation in time, we shall be able to say with confidence that all these demands would be accepted. The third might indeed have been carried out by a commander-in-chief in General MacArthur's position and fortified by his immense prestige without permission from anyone.

It was realization of what total war involved,

especially in the nuclear age, that was responsible for the restraint. It may indeed be reasonable to find in it a welcome feature of the Korean War. The new moderation was not a sign of cowardice, as it then appeared to many of General MacArthur's supporters. It was a statesmanlike decision to withhold the full weight of the chastisement merited by a people guilty of criminal conduct, for the sake of humanity in general. Though the policy had to face considerable hostility at the time in the United States, it has since been almost universally accepted as correct. And yet, what the United States Joint Chiefs of Staff said to General MacArthur when informing him that his retaliatory measures could not be permitted was startling, though it has now been conveniently forgotten. They told him that, rather than use the means he was asking for, he should abandon the peninsula if that step appeared necessary for the safety of his forces.[10]

Events in Korea were, however, influenced by the fact that it was not regarded as a conflict of the very highest importance. Victory could not be pursued until the point was reached at which it might set alight the combustible material with which the world was laden. The effort to attain victory could not be pressed until the resources which would be required in a major and vital war had been dangerously depleted. As Clausewitz has pointed out, where the stakes are not high efforts are likely to be diminished and when one of the belligerents faces adversity it may decide to accept conditions of a kind which it would indignantly

[10] Falls, *A Hundred Years of War*, p. 390.

reject in a life-and-death struggle. Thoughtful observers of events in Korea decided glumly that they
might not prove as promising a precedent as looked
likely at first glance. When issues are great they are
apt to take control. Men are swept along by them and
the voices of the prudent are unheard.

It is a commonplace that total war in the nuclear age
represents the greatest peril with which mankind has
ever been faced. So obvious is the fact that a concept of
restraint has entered even this field. Apart from the
pleas, the schemes, and the demonstrations of un-
official bodies and individuals—some of the theses
respectable by reason of their ingenuity but subject to
the disadvantage that those who make them do not bear
responsibility for the defence of their countries and
may not be fully informed—the desire for restraint has
spread to governments. There is good reason to believe
that here the sentiments of Soviet Russia approach
those of the United States, the United Kingdom, and
other democratic nations. More and more we gain the
impression that nuclear warfare has been relegated to
a last resort, to avoid which great efforts will be made.
It still remains an imbecility to place complete reliance
on the familiar phrase: 'the megaton bomb is now
unlikely to be used'. Another saying, that 'we shall
have to live with it for some time yet', is more to the
point. Only genuine reductions in output and 'means
of delivery' on both sides can begin a movement towards safety.

Chapter Nine

AIR FORCES AS HANDMAIDS, DESPOTS, AND UNDER CHALLENGE

At the outbreak of the First World War in 1914 the strongest air force in the world, that of Germany, numbered 384 aeroplanes. In proportion to the strength of land forces, however, the British Expeditionary Force had by far the largest number of aeroplanes, a total of sixty-three. By comparison with the aircraft of a mere thirty years later these types appear children's toys—slats of wood, strips of canvas, glue and wire. Their maximum speed rarely reached 70 miles an hour. They were adjuncts of the armies. The British force was a 'corps' (Royal Flying Corps), in the same sense as the Royal Engineers. A few weeks before the outbreak of war the Naval Wing had been taken out—broken away in fact—and become the Royal Naval Air Service. Where both services were concerned the role of air forces was reconnaissance. No more was required of them. They occasionally carried very small bombs which they dropped over the side. In the phase of open warfare pilots brought in some useful reports of hostile movements and would have achieved more but for the screen of forests in full leaf.

The growth of the air forces in size, speed, range, versatility, and functions, especially in the first quality, was striking. When trench warfare set in on the

Western Front reconnaissance, still important, became less vital, though in Poland, Russia, and Galicia it largely maintained its place. Static warfare called for new duties. The two first and more or less simultaneously undertaken were photography of the enemy's defences and the ranging of artillery by wireless. The whole trench system from the Channel to the Swiss frontier was traced on maps with complete accuracy. Photography was later on used for another purpose in country such as Macedonia where the existing maps were deficient. Ground behind the front could be mapped by the normal processes of survey, but it was valuable to obtain a rough knowledge of that in the enemy's hands from photographs and translate these into conventionalized contours.

To start with the only weapons carried were rifles or even revolvers. When, however, photographic and artillery co-operation missions became common it was natural that fighting for mastery should follow. Machine guns were taken into use. Special anti-aircraft batteries were formed. At the end of 1915 the Germans introduced the Fokker monoplane with the propeller in front and an 'interrupter' gear which synchronized the flow of the machine gun bullets with the engine, so that they passed between the blades.[1] Now began the great days of the 'ace' fighter pilots, whose exploits created ardent interest and admiration. Men such as the Frenchman Charles Guynemer, the Briton Albert Ball, and the German Max Immelmann became the supreme heroes of their nations. They were certainly among the

[1] Jones, *The War in the Air*, Vol. ii, p. 149.

most skilled practitioners of the art of war. Fighting to destroy or protect aircraft engaged on other missions or for command of the air in general continued to the end of the war. In the later stages 'dog-fights' occurred in which a hundred or more aircraft took part.

Meanwhile, aircraft capable of carrying much heavier bombs had appeared. Generally speaking, bombing by day proved ineffective except during periods when the side practising it ruled the skies. It was used with great effect in pursuit of beaten foes in the final campaigns in outer theatres, especially in Macedonia and Palestine. Night bombing was harder to fight and became of considerable value. In some cases, such as the breaking of Austrian pontoon bridges on the Piave, bombing was crucial. In 1918 the British formed an 'independent' air force to attack Germany, but it never got into its stride. Its De Havilland day bombers had a speed of 120 miles an hour and could carry nearly 600 lb. weight of bombs. On Armistice Day Britain had over 3,000 first-line aircraft in France and Belgium.

The Germans, who were far ahead of any rival in the science of lighter-than-air construction, refused to accept the general belief that the future lay entirely with the heavier-than-air. Their Zeppelins—and other types usually classed under the same generic title— were employed chiefly in night attacks on England. On one occasion a single airship did a million pounds worth of damage in a raid, but on the whole their success was mainly moral and measured in terms of absenteeism in factories and sensational drops in the production of warlike material. In the end the alliance of the defence and the weather drove the Zeppelins out of the skies and in fact destroyed most of them.

The Royal Naval Air Service and naval aircraft in general had to face the conflict with equipment which, though comparable to that of the Royal Flying Corps, was not far enough advanced to be of much service in the more difficult element of the sea. The R.N.A.S. did magnificent work in the Gallipoli campaign, of which it assumed the whole burden. In the earlier phases the lack of range was a crippling handicap and even when this was partially removed the vulnerability of the aircraft to stormy weather at sea remained. The second handicap kept the force almost entirely out of naval actions, but it played a part of increasing value in anti-submarine warfare. Britain brought into service the first aircraft-carriers by converting ships built for other purposes, and the *Ark Royal* reached the scene at the beginning of the Gallipoli campaign. The *Engadine* sailed with the battle cruisers to the Battle of Jutland, but exercised no effect. Aircraft could take off from the decks of carriers but could not land on them. They therefore had to alight on the water and to be raised by a crane, so that prospects of recovery were indifferent unless the water was calm. The first deck-landing, on the *Furious*, did not occur until 2 August 1917, and even then the aircraft was actually pulled down by rope toggles.[2] Seaplanes, which could alight on the water on floats, were also used.

On 1 April 1918, Britain created the Royal Air Force,

[2] Jones, *The War in the Air*, Vol. iv, p. 27.

after setting up an Air Ministry earlier in the year. The three air forces were combined. Where operations in the field were concerned the change made little difference. The commanders in the field conformed to the wishes of the commanders-in-chief of the land forces as faithfully as they had obeyed their orders. The new title marked the growing importance of air forces and looked forward to their future. The man on whose advice the R.A.F. had been formed, General Smuts, wrote in his report: 'As far as can at present be foreseen there is absolutely no limit to the scale of its future independent war use.'[3] Though the wartime commanders still in general used their forces as components of the two older services, as soon as the war was over they naturally began to assert their independence. No other state imitated the United Kingdom, though during the next twenty years all the major air forces made some advance towards autonomy.

Peace was in most respects more favourable than war to aircraft development. People pressed for time began to make long trips, for example, from South Africa to Croydon, with several nights spent at stops in East Africa, and perhaps taking to a flying boat in the Mediterranean. An unfortunate aspect was the general unwillingness to spend more than the minimum on military equipment. This had the result that, while vast improvements were made, the democratic countries ordered sparingly and retained numbers of obsolete and virtually useless aircraft up to the outbreak of the Second World War and after it. Civilian flying

[3] Ibid., Vol. vi, pp. 5-12.

aided the development of military, and, whereas early in the First World War it was considered remarkable that single-seater aircraft could be flown across the Channel from England to France, relatively early in the Second World War bombers were flown across the Atlantic.

Peace was also a period of conflict between the two old services and the young one. The Air Ministry had to fight for its life and that of the R.A.F. There was in the early days talk of abolishing both. Their counter-attack was pressed hard. Successes were gained. Above all, the R.A.F. maintained its independence. It assumed a certain independent role in imperial defence. It stalled effectively for a long time against the Navy's attempt to recover its own air arm, not yielding until June 1937, disastrously late in the day from the naval point of view. A similar division of functions was made by other air forces. The struggle was often bitter, but the result is now accepted as a matter of course and the arrangement is undoubtedly correct.

The ideas of the Air Ministry and of nearly all senior R.A.F. officers were founded on the assumption that the air represented the predominant realm in warfare, that it was the predestined war-winner. They were apt to look upon the demands of the Admiralty and War Office for co-operative efforts as attempts to divert them from their proper role. Their supporters now say they were 'in advance of their time' and take this as eulogy. Yet being in advance of one's time may be as fatal as being behind it if it leads to going to war with a fallacious doctrine. The Fleet Air Arm fought with inadequate aircraft till far into the war. The

Army was starved for lack of air support, partly because rearmament came so late but partly through concentration on heavy bombers.

Early in the war the German armies owed much in their victories in Poland, Belgium, and France to their dive-bombers. These aircraft acted in close support to the armour and infantry. In some cases during the breaking of the French front on the Meuse they replaced the artillery, most of which had been outpaced. They often put hostile artillery out of action, but generally by driving the detachments from their guns. The successes were won for the most part by moral rather than material effect. To troops unused to them, especially the French divisions of low categories, they proved extremely unsettling. The aircraft were in fact highly vulnerable both from the ground and from the air. This fact was not, however, fully recognized to start with because the defending troops, not well equipped with anti-aircraft weapons, became too shaken to make use of them and because the Germans won the command of the air at an early stage. Dive-bombers were to gain further triumphs, but their importance diminished. This was probably a case in which Air Ministry policy was correct. It resisted a press campaign for fleets of dive-bombers for the British Army with success. The fighter-bomber was to prove more effective and far more versatile.

The next great struggle was very different. In the Battle of Britain which began in early August 1940 it may be said that, despite the value of anti-aircraft weapons and devices, air force was pitted against air force, 'grappling in the central blue'. On the decision depended the fate of Britain, and it was because the R.A.F. was victorious that the German naval and military commands failed to bring about the conditions they considered to be the prerequisites of invasion and finally called it off. In this phase the aspirations of the 'air-minded' were fulfilled because the enemy forced the issue—but the bomber was utterly defeated in day-fighting.

The attackers were then forced to turn to night-bombing. To start with they had things almost all their own way. The defence was not strong in night-fighting; radar had only begun its development; and the bombers kept above the height at which searchlights could illuminate them and well above the balloons. The anti-aircraft artillery got virtually no targets. The defence gradually improved its situation and the losses of the bombers increased. The damage done continued to be very heavy, however, and loss of life, suffering, and the handicap to production were serious. Viewed from the most important outlook of all, Britain's survival, the switch from day-bombing was a benefit. This was small consolation for the cities, some of which were tem-porarily paralysed, while the whole centre of a small one, Coventry, was destroyed. It was fortunate for Britain that, when Hitler decided to invade Russia, he had to close down the bomber offensive in the spring of 1941.

Meanwhile Britain, whose small expeditionary force had been compelled to abandon continental Europe by the defeat and occupation of her allies, had no means of striking back except with bombers, and that on a very minor scale. The early effects were negligible. If, however, the policy was to be what it officially became, that of breaking the spirit of the German people by bombing objectives representing whole cities, or in the case of vast cities large sections of them, then it was obviously right to begin as soon as possible. The blows reached a frightful intensity by the last year of the war. They were duplicated by those of the United States Army Air Force struck by day. Their bombers carried a lighter load of bombs but were faster and more strongly armed. The first results indicated that the Flying Fortresses and Liberators could take care of themselves with their numerous large-calibre machine guns. However, German fighter tactics improved and the aircraft were increasingly armed with cannon. The balance was dramatically reversed. American losses rose rapidly till they became almost unbearable. There was, however, no question of admitting defeat. Fighters carrying spare petrol tanks now began to escort the bombers, so that once again they could carry out day-bombing without excessive loss.

In function apart from performance—though the advance here was sensational also—the most remarkable development was in naval aircraft, especially carrier-borne. Of the British victories at Taranto and Cape Matapan, the first was gained entirely by carrier-borne torpedo-bombers and the second developed from the stopping of an Italian cruiser by one.

Far more striking still, because on such a vastly greater scale, were the exploits of the American and

Japanese carriers and their aircraft in the Pacific. In the prolonged campaigns of this ocean there occurred a number of ship-to-ship battles, some of them highly important, in which neither carriers nor even aircraft played any part, but all the great battles were in the main or wholly carrier battles. It was on the basis of his victories in these that Admiral Nimitz made his advance on Japan. Army Air Forces indeed participated, but their part in the progress of Nimitz was a minor one until they began to strike from the Marianas, to which sea power, including naval air power, had brought them. It was an extraordinary triumph for the concept of carrier warfare and above all for the specialists in it, such as Admiral Marc Mitscher.

The future of carriers provides matter for argument. Wholly contradictory views about it are held by experienced and thinking men, and legitimately so. Denigration of their achievement in the Pacific is, however, childish. The extent to which service rivalry may colour intelligent minds appears in the comment of one of the ablest senior officers of the R.A.F. in modern times and one feeling deep affection for the sister services, Marshal of the Royal Air Force Sir John Slessor.

'It was the misfortune of the British and American taxpayer that the late war ended in a blaze of glory for the aircraft-carrier in a Pacific campaign before the advent of the guided atom bomb, against Air Forces which, while admirably brave, were so inefficient that they had to fall back upon the forlorn expedient of *Kamikaze.*'

Now the Japanese Naval Air Force was very far

from inefficient until the United States Naval Air Force
had worn it out by shooting down its best airmen or
sunk the carriers while the aircraft were in the air—
two birds with one stone. The early achievement
of Japanese pilots and carriers was good. Time
to train more equally good pilots was not allowed. Of
British air forces the writer remarks: 'I cannot call to
mind any warlike action against an enemy maritime
objective carried out by a naval aircraft from a carrier
that was not done more often and just as effectively by
an R.A.F. aircraft from a base on the shore.'[4]

Well, at Cape Matapan, R.A.F. aircraft from bases
on the shore tried more often than Fleet Air Arm
aircraft from carriers (and a few from an airfield in
Crete). The net results were: twenty-four naval sorties
got two torpedo hits on the Italian fleet. The final
result of one of them was the sinking of three armoured
cruisers and two destroyers. Thirty R.A.F. bomber
sorties achieved no hits.[5] It may be said that the naval
aircraft were more suitable than those of the R.A.F.,
but surely this is part of the case for a naval air service.
And it would be interesting to learn which were the
occasions when R.A.F. aircraft performed 'more often
and just as effectively' tasks similar to those of the attack
on Taranto or the hit which jammed the *Bismarck's*
rudder and led to the destruction of the great battleship.

This criticism comes from the pen of a writer whose
modest service in war was that of a soldier, whose
nearest senior naval kinsman died a century and a half

[4] Slessor, *The Central Blue*, pp. 191, 192.
[5] Roskill, *The War at Sea*, Vol. i, map 35.

ago, and who has never been aboard a carrier. He hopes that these antecedents ensure a certain objectivity where independent and naval air forces are in question. In studying the decisive Battle of the Philippine Sea, fought on 19 and 20 June 1944, he has been deeply impressed, not only by 'the skill, initiative, and intrepid courage' of the American airmen, but also by 'the brainwork of the combat information centres in tracking Japanese raids, and of fighter-directors in arranging interceptions; the energy of deck crews in rapid-fire launching, recovery, and servicing of planes; the accuracy of battle-line anti-aircraft gunners'.[6] He finds it hard to believe that an independent service, a service not trained and integrated within the Navy, not thinking and living for naval air war and at the same time prepared for all its many variations, a service whose reflexes did not respond in a flash to the significance of a fleeting and for all others insignificant scene—that such a service could have produced the results of 'the Great Marianas Turkey Shoot'.

The fighter-bomber was primarily the auxiliary of the armies, though German fighter-bombers were used with considerable material and greater moral effect by the Germans against London, to keep the pot boiling until the flying bombs were ready. As regards land campaigns and battles the opposing forces did not meet on an equality in this form of attack. By the time the British and American fighter-bomber forces became strong, well-organized, and well-trained, their German equivalents had shrunk in power.

[6] Morison, *New Guinea and the Marianas*, p. 278.

This was one of the most valuable results of the bombing policy which not only hampered production but compelled Germany to concentrate on the production, organization, and training of night-fighter aircraft and pilots. American and British industrial strength had by 1944 and even to a considerable extent by 1943 become capable of meeting all demands, so that land armies were richly provided with tactical air support from fighter-bombers. It is well known that in many fields of industry as well as in war controversy about the use of material dies down as soon as there is enough for all. The American and British tactical air forces became linked into teams with the land armies and quickly acquired the speed of thought and skill in execution of orders which only experience can produce.

Another co-operative effort between the staffs and troops of land and air is to be found in airborne forces. These were of two kinds: parachute forces dropped from aircraft in flight, and forces which were landed, frequently by gliders towed by aircraft. For obvious reasons, when airborne forces were to be established behind a hostile front and likely to have to fight from the start, the parachutists were dropped first. Their disadvantage was that, even when the circumstances were favourable and the pilots at their most skilful, the parachutists were apt to be so scattered in their drop that concentration was difficult. A relatively small error or accident might result in their being dropped so far from the area intended that their chance of securing the landing-place for the gliders was diminished or disappeared altogether. On the other hand, towed gliders were vulnerable in the extreme.

Step by step, the organization of these forces was built up. Special weapons and equipment which could also be dropped by parachute were provided. The dropping of food, which had been practised on a few occasions in the First World War, had by now become a commonplace and was carried out on a large scale in normal as well as in airborne warfare. The most clear-cut success was the capture of Crete by the Germans with airborne forces alone. They were used by the Americans and British in great strength on three occasions in the final invasion of North-West Europe: to assist the original landings in the Bay of the Seine, to jump the great water barriers in Southern Holland, and to play a part in the passage of the Rhine. For various reasons, however, the part played by airborne forces was rather smaller than had seemed probable. Large numbers of German parachutists fought as normal infantry. The Russians, the pioneers in this field, exploited it little.

The transport of troops and supplies by air exercised a great influence on strategy and even tactics. It is best exemplified by the campaigns in Burma. During the Japanese invasion of Assam a whole division was moved up by air from the Arakan and a second brought partly by air from Bengal. In the British advance more than one column was able to use a route along which it could not have been supplied by road—there was indeed virtually no road—because supplies of all natures were carried by air. It should also be noted that this was densely forested country

full of roving bands of Japanese soldiers. To have
kept open a long line of communication would
thus have been difficult and would have used up
large numbers of troops. Air supply thus gave
the columns freedom of action and economized in
man-power.

We return to the subject of strategic bombing for
the last stage of the war. It had now risen enormously.
Targets varied with circumstances: one month they
might be railways, the next oil. Yet it can be fairly
said that the target which was generally given priority
over all others was—Berlin. It was not only the capital
of Germany but, by reason of its processing and
finishing industries, of very high significance to the
German war effort.[7] Other objectives constantly
engaged were Hamburg and the Ruhr towns, but there
was hardly a town of the slightest industrial importance that was not visited. The destruction in Berlin
and many other cities and towns was inconceivable.
Those who saw it shortly after the cessation of hostilities were, however, equally shocked by the appearance
of the yellow-faced, shabby, sickly inhabitants. All
serious activity must surely, one would have thought,
have been brought to an end a long time before.
Not so. The extraordinary fact remains that the
German industrial output for 1944 was the highest of
the war. As for the theory that German war industry
could be destroyed by the demoralization of the
workers, it failed because, as a general rule, the workers
refused to be demoralized. It would seem that the

[7] Falls, *The Second World War*, p. 211.

British loss of output from absenteeism during the attacks by V1's and V2's was higher than that of Germany at any time in 1944.

The effects are much clearer in the case of Japan than in that of Germany. After the big American Army Air Force bombers had been provided with bases within effective bombing range of Japan they battered the country into surrender. The atomic bombs may have hastened the surrender somewhat but were in no sense its cause. By the end of the war, then, bombing had become the predominant weapon, to a certain extent because it was actually so, for the rest because most people thought it was. The makers of the bombing policies could not well renounce their theories when they came to write their books.

After the war aircraft continued to grow bigger, faster, and immensely more costly. Yet development tended to be slower. So much research, discussion, and experiment was involved in the production of a new type that from the drawing-board stage it might take six years before it appeared in numbers. The Korean War showed once more that machinery had not yet done away with the advantage of brains, skill, and training. The fighting was almost entirely between fighter aircraft of nearly comparable performance on both sides. The American pilots, however, held the advantage throughout, even though often outnumbered.

Unquestioned dominance of air power was coincident with the termination of the war. On 6 August 1945 the first atomic bomb was dropped and on 9 August the second; on 10 August Japan sued for peace. Thus, whereas up to the end there remained room for discussion, whereas one school might declare that vast land armies of invasion had been necessary to bring Germany to her knees and another might assert that the main blows had been dealt by bombers and that they could have brought about the final result without the aid of armies if they had been allowed to expand at the expense of armies, the atomic bomb had now become the ultimate weapon. It was the weapon of the bomber aircraft. Therefore the bomber aircraft was supreme.

It is true that as time passed what had appeared a simple situation was discovered to be in fact one of high complexity. The power of atomic weapons was multiplied. It was revealed that their effects were not confined to the force of their explosions but included those of vaporous dust which they left floating in the air, capable of covering vast distances and of infecting mankind with deadly and incurable diseases transmitted to offspring. The possibility—and hope—that the holders of these weapons would recoil from their use became greater. Still, even if the bomb was never to be used, it was there and the means of delivery was still the aircraft. Then, however, a challenge to the dominance of air power which had nothing to do with morality or the desire for survival appeared in the distance. It was the long-range guided missile, fired from a site on the ground.

Of course, as generally happens in such cases, the

early prophets underestimated the length of time that would be required to perfect these instruments. If, however, we proceed on the hateful assumption that nuclear weapons remain, it is a matter of relatively small importance whether the means by which they are delivered are revolutionized in three years, or six, or nine. So far as can at present be foreseen, air forces will lose this function. (They will stake out claims to missile bases, but the sections on such tasks will be 'air forces' only by courtesy.) Air power will lose its dominance and the aircraft will cease to be the most essential piece of military equipment. Air forces cannot go back to their old role of despatching fleets of heavy bombers carrying bombs of 1,000 lb. or more against their country's foes because this would be the surest way to bring on a nuclear war. If nuclear weapons remain, long-range missiles will become paramount. The process could be stopped only by a method of identifying their sites so surely that these could be overwhelmed by a surprise attack.

Simultaneously, however, there appeared another complex development of the possibilities of the future and therefore of military thought. The more likely it was that the ghastly ultimate weapon would be held back, the more likely it became that occasional small wars with 'conventional' weapons would occur. Now this was interesting and important for many nations, but for none so significant as for the United Kingdom, the senior partner in a Commonwealth scattered over the world and bearing heavy responsibilities for the defence of colonies and mandates. For Britain the most

probable kind of conflict to be envisaged and prepared for in equipment programmes was a combined
operation involving all three services. From the point
of view of the Fleet Air Arm it meant that the carrier,
large or small, seemed certain to be the Navy's most
suitable contribution to a 'task-force' operating in the
three elements of land, sea, and air. So the future of
naval aircraft seemed well assured, always taking into
account the unpredictable changes which make
defence ministers age prematurely. At the same time
the demand for air transport, particularly on the part
of the Army, increased. The Army was, within less
than ten years from the end of the war, undergoing a
second sharp reduction, but the nation was promised
that it would be made extremely mobile, not only as
regards men but in the transportation of considerable
amounts of equipment.

The position is therefore that air forces are threatened
by the loss of functions which for a brief period gave
them single-handed performance, but that new opportunities simultaneously beckon to them. The phases of
their career over a period of a little over a half a
century may, if these assumptions are correct, be
described in terms of their relations with the other
services as: handmaids (1914–18)—rivals (1918–45)—
autocrats (1945–?65)—partners. There is no reason to
fear that they will become handmaids once again. They
are well enough established to be secure against such
a calamity. Defence by service-partnership, tactically
as well as strategically, is the healthiest system. It is
one which has existed between the Royal Navy and

the Army for centuries and has never been broken
except by squabbles, the majority of which have had
prize money as their basis. In the present circumstances
the signs point to the desirability of its embracing all
the forces of the Crown.

Chapter Ten

STRATEGY AND TACTICS OF
THE SECOND WORLD WAR

STRATEGY

THE most powerful army in the Second World War was controlled by a man who had served as a lance-corporal and messenger or 'runner' in the First. That war made an indelible impression upon him, but spiritually alone, not strategically or tactically, still less administratively. He had little conception of problems of maintenance; none at all of naval operations. Yet from that tortured and diseased mind emanated flashes of genius, especially in the earlier stages. Sometimes these led to plans and blows which were extremely successful, though they scared his military commanders and advisers. Chief of these is the conquest of Norway where he faced enormous risks. There was no room in his composition, however, for the unspectacular but valuable ingredient of common sense, any more than for humanity. When the Germans entered the Ukraine in 1941 they were regarded as liberators. The first battles and the mass surrenders suggested that the Russian troops were far from enthusiastic. Some senior officers came over to the Germans. What a soil to cultivate! Hitler, however, looked upon the Slavs as '*Untermenschen*, fit only for slave labour'. More than that, he had made up his mind to exterminate a large proportion of the population between the Vistula and the Urals to make way for German and Germanic colonists.[1] He thus became one of the architects of German defeat in the East.

Hitler had a good eye for a brilliant plan so long as it did not involve yielding a yard of ground at any point. The plan by means of which France was overthrown in 1940 was conceived by Manstein, then a staff officer, but Hitler adopted it. One may say that he was a far better offensive than defensive strategist. Above all, he thought in grandiose terms. To a large extent, owing to new found mobility and the range of aircraft, this was true of many planners, and had to be. Certainly there was no lack of amplitude in the conceptions of his principal foe, Winston Churchill. Hitler, however, was a behemoth in strategy even in a war of behemoths, and German operations reflected his image.

Before dealing with the war as a whole let us glance at one state with great military traditions whose share in it *as a nation* ended in the summer of 1940. French strategy was wholly defensive. Some vague projects of turning to the offensive when the right time came were discussed, as were pin-pricks in south-eastern Europe, but this was largely talk. The dominating factor in French strategy, perhaps in most cases unconscious, was the concept of keeping war as far as possible from the French people and to this end doing the minimum of fighting. Clausewitz said that when the motives of one

[1] Bullock, *Hitler, a Study in Tyranny*, pp. 633, 637. Fuller, *The Decisive Battles*, Vol. iii, pp. 434-7.

belligerent are strong and the will to give battle determined, whereas on the other side the desire is for a
moderate war not calling for a supreme effort, victory
is likely to go to the former. It is, moreover, a mistake
to suppose that sacrifice can ultimately be avoided by a
policy of the defensive at all costs. The one bold feature
of French strategy was the advance to the Dyle position
as soon as the Germans invaded Belgium. It was in a
sense strategic offensive with tactical defensive, a
method immortalized by Wellington—but he had
exceptionally steady and straight-shooting troops. The
French played into Hitler's hands by emerging into
the open.

If British strategy was less spectacular than German,
it extended over wider fields; in fact, with that of the
United States after that country had entered the war,
it encircled the globe. The original British strategic
ideas were nullified by the fall of France. The next
development was based—very speculatively based,
since the offensive against the Italians was a series of
steps in the dark—on typical British policy, that of
striking at an enemy in a relatively hedged-in theatre
of war for want of anything more promising. It was to
clear the coast of North Africa, mainly in order to keep
open the Mediterranean. The Germans came to the
aid of Italy, with the consequence that Britain's task
took her nearly two and a half years and involved
grave rebuffs before it was completed with American
aid. It was always war in three elements, sea, land,
and air.

Meanwhile, Japan had entered the war, put the

American Pacific Fleet out of action and quickly
overrun Malaya, the Netherlands East Indies, and
presently Burma, while holding American power at a
distance. The Australian forces in the Middle East and
Europe were brought back to defend their own country
in New Guinea. Again it was war in three elements on
both sides. Henceforth the offensive strategy of the
kind which Britain would have liked to use against
the Japanese was emasculated to supply the needs of
the Middle East and Europe, and it took the remainder
of the war to retake Burma and Malaya overland.
British seapower had in the past been over-strained,
but never to this extent.

Britain was unable to formulate a bold and strong
strategy until the United States had become a belligerent. One principle on which the new allies agreed was
that the defeat of Germany should have priority over the
defeat of Japan. A second was that the decisive blows
against Germany must be struck through Northern
France. A third was the importance of the bombing of
Germany. Invasion through France having been ruled
out in 1942 and 1943, the British again chose a secondary and partially self-contained theatre—Italy. The
United States agreed unenthusiastically. However, the
power of the United States was now expanding to such
an extent that the last word on strategy was always
hers. Government and command turned down the
British proposal of a thrust into the valley of the
Danube from Italy and in the hour of victory rejected
that of pressing east to secure the political objectives
of Berlin and Prague. Within the means at Britain's

disposal and measured by the influence she could bring to bear Britain's strategy was typical and in general good. Where it was nullified or modified, some good American opinion has since decided that Britain was right.

The names 'Berlin' and 'Prague' remind us of the deep distrust which the actions of Russia aroused in British minds some time before the war was over. Few nations can ever have fought a war with political objectives in a more prominent place on the programme. Whereas Russian military strategy was conventional and even commonplace, political strategy was novel and imaginative. On the military side the Russian aim was to wear the enemy out by the use of vastly superior numbers and equipment, continually switching the fighting and running the German reserves off their feet. (The finest achievement of all, at Stalingrad, was based on an obvious strategy and might well have been better managed in the execution.) The political strategy aimed at the seizure of Rumania, Bulgaria, Hungary, Czechoslovakia, and Eastern Germany, their bolshevization and the extermination of most or all the 'capitalists' and intelligentsia, and their establishment as outposts and buffers. By their means Russia would be provided with shock-absorbers against invasion, assembly places on which Russian armies of invasion might hope to be less heavily bombed than on their own soil and would be in good positions for quick action, and screens against inquisitive eyes, which the Communist leaders then dreaded. Whether or not this policy was in any case destined to succeed as the result of Russian victory is uncertain. What is certain is that the persistent belief of the United States Government that, in its own idiom, Russia was ready to 'play ball', favoured the real Russian policy.

What has been said of British and Russian strategy must suffice to cover American strategy in Europe. The Pacific is another matter. There American brains, resource, skill, equipment, and administrative improvisation were brilliant. Combined operations were far from novelites, and 'island hopping' had been carried out before the days of steam or aircraft. This, however, was a field so vast and involving so many new factors that the problems faced by the great commanders, MacArthur and Nimitz, had to be solved *ab initio*. The success of their cogitations is beyond dispute. The only doubtful point is the judgement of the Joint Chiefs of Staff when they had to decide between the rival schemes of the two commanders-in-chief for the advance on Japan: Nimitz taking over the main effort, skipping out the reconquest of the Philippines, and establishing long-range army bombers on sites from which they were expected to pound Japan into surrender; or MacArthur striking through the Philippines, and in the process cutting Japan off from the supplies of oil, rubber, tin, and rice on which she depended. The solution was a compromise, slightly favouring Nimitz. Two lines of advance were maintained.[2] Opinion is divided on the subject, but each line played so valuable a part that it was probably right to move on both.

[2] Moriso∷, *New Guinea and the Marianas*, pp. 1–10. Willoughby, *MacArthur*, pp. 218–22.

Broadly speaking, the advance was carried out on the principle of seizing desirable objectives, particularly as air bases, and by-passing those which were less valuable and in which Japanese garrisons could be nullified from the air and by submarines. But war, as Napoleon said, is 'all in the execution'. The intellectual power and precision in the working out of this principle was tremendous.

What of the victim? Japan's war plan was brilliant so far as it went, but ended in a void. It was probably the most ambitious scheme of conquest up to date. 'She intended to destroy the United States Pacific Fleet, to capture the Philippines, Borneo, Malaya, the Netherlands East Indies and Burma, and to establish east of them an impregnable ring of ocean fortresses, through Wake, the Marshall Islands, and the archipelago north of Australia. Behind this barrier she would be able to transfer the riches of the conquests to the home country and fill the gaps in her economy.'[3] Stupendous—but what then? All this and more was accomplished. Yet there was no logical follow-up, no decision. The only rags of a policy were hopes that *when* British sea power had been destroyed by herself and Germany, and *when* Russia had been forced by the latter to sue for peace, the United States would find it impossible to continue the war. The Japanese Navy would do all in its power to support the programme by bringing on a fleet battle. It attained this end more than once, but not the battleship conflict for which it longed.

[3] Falls, *A Hundred Years of War*, p. 353.

The turning point was the Battle of Midway in June 1942; the most decisive defeat suffered by Japan was the Battle of the Philippine Sea in July 1944, in which three of her carriers were sunk—two by submarines— and the core of her carrier-borne air fleet destroyed. Aircraft carriers dominated the fighting in the Pacific. The supreme dominating factor was, however, the superiority of American industrial output, the total being ten times as great as that of Japan and, let us say, four-tenths of this total being used against Japan.

The same tale, with a different background, has to be told of the defeat of Germany. To put it inelegantly, Germany and Japan both bit off more than they could chew. Both nevertheless made their contributions, like the victorious powers, Britain, the United States, and Russia, to the prodigious distances covered by offensives. The only one of the First World War which challenges the great offensives of the Second is that of the Germans and Austrians which began at Gorlice in May 1915 and covered a maximum of some 350 miles that year. The mobility provided by armour, aircraft, and fast-moving transport had transformed conditions between the two wars and brought the offensive into the ascendant to as great an extent as field fortification had put the defensive into the ascendant in the earlier war.

Yet, once again, sea power had proved decisive. What, it may be asked, of the bomber offensive against Germany? The simple answer is that every drop of the oil used came by sea.

TACTICS

The tactics of the Second World War were as diverse as the theatres. Even where the combatants did not to begin with recognize that tactics must be moulded to conform to the terrain, experience taught them that this was the basis of success. Well-roaded country, whether industrialized, agricultural, or both, as in France and Germany; deserts of rock, gravel, and sand, as in North Africa; open plains, as in Poland and Russia; corridors on the flanks of a vast mountain spine, which threw out hilly ribs and deep-cut rivers to the coast, as in Italy; jungles, forests, and plantations, as in Malaya and Burma; primitive islands and atolls, as in the Pacific; completely mountainous country, as in Western Ethiopia: all these called for different methods of fighting. As always since the growth of armies in the mid-nineteenth century, tactics as well as strategy were influenced by the means of supply. Again as history indicated, the more primitive the ordinary life of the people, the less the influence of supply. The Japanese soldier with his rice and dried fruit, the Russian cavalryman feeding his horse on the thatch of a house, were freer to fight as they chose than the American.

The most successful tactics were, however, characterized by daring, by exploiting the effect of the unexpected. The Japanese infantry battalion slipping round a flank and establishing a deadly road-block in the enemy's rear was exploiting new ideas almost as much as the German tank regiment splitting the enemy's front and cutting his communications. The new weapons and equipment favoured the tactical as well as the strategic offensive.

The German victory in France was gained mainly by the alliance of armour and aircraft. In proportion to the speed and endurance of the tanks—if intelligently maintained and supplied with fuel and lubricant, as the German armoured forces were—the depth of the country from the Ardennes to the Channel was no greater than could be covered by a single thrust. The fact that it would not have been crossed thus if the tank commanders had not taken matters into their own hands is beside the point. This thrust which drove a corridor right through the allied array to the sea is misunderstood if regarded only in the light of strategy, as if all that were necessary was good planning. It depended on tactics at every step. It was based on the prospect that the Germans would outfight the French at every step, as they did in fact. It is true that the ease and rapidity of their 'victory without a morrow' were so great that it astonished even the most optimistic, but they had counted on tactical victory. They won not merely through their organization, under which the armoured division was made independent of the infantry, but through the way they fought their tanks.

The problem was altogether different in Russia. Here space was unlimited in breadth and depth. The vast breadth meant that infantry would have to play a far greater part than in France. The vast depth in front of the German armies called for the invention of objectives short of the final one of Moscow. The solution was found in convergent thrusts, the inner

DIAGRAM V

SECOND WORLD WAR: SURPRISE ATTACK GAZALA, 27 MAY 1942

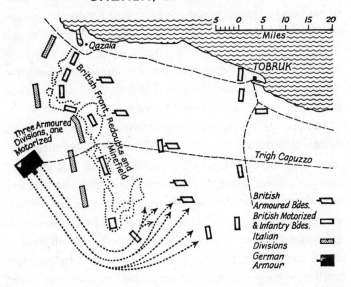

flanks of which might be as much as 50 miles apart at the outset. The supreme example of these major tactics is the Battle of Viasma-Briansk in October 1941. These twin convergent offensives netted upwards of 700,000 prisoners and 5,500 guns. Again it was the speed, boldness, and fighting qualities of the Panzer divisions which formed the basis of this unexampled victory, but the contribution of the fast-marching infantry was greater than in France. Again the Luftwaffe played an indispensable part.

In this phase Russian tactics were clumsy in the extreme. Attacks were made blindly and defence was never organized. When the Russians had had time to assemble their strength and establish a great numerical superiority they developed their own tactics. They were particularly good at infiltration and the seizure of bridgeheads over rivers as first steps to an offensive. They used their tanks in mass, supported by massed artillery—they themselves regarded artillery as their finest arm. They became bolder with success, but rarely emulated the thrusts of a Guderian or a Hoth. Their tactics remained essentially based on superior strength.

The oft-quoted saying that the North African desert was 'the paradise of the tactician and the nightmare of the quartermaster' is true. The country was hard on tanks but they could go anywhere, with the exception that they could mount or descend the famous escarpment only at points where established roads or tracks crossed it. Thus the fighting was armoured warfare in its pure and fundamental form. For all their traditions, the British, the pioneers of the tank, had a lot to learn from the Germans, and it was not until greatly superior strength in armour and men had been brought into the theatre that they were able to win a decisive victory. One of the tactical devices of their most skilful foe, Erwin Rommel, laid the foundations of defeat upon defeat for the British. When counter-attacked he would form a hidden screen of anti-tank artillery—in which the German armoured forces were strong and efficient—and contrive to lure the British tanks into its short-range fire. He exercised personal control from a command vehicle throughout all his battles and was, German critics said, too often absent from his headquarters—but it paid on balance.

The other great desert tactician, Montgomery, who defeated him, was more cautious by temperament and in practice. Yet, coming, like Rommel before him, fresh to the terrain—though as a battalion commander he had trained a battalion of infantry in Sinai—he displayed complete understanding of its tactical possibilities from the first. At Alamein, in his prolonged struggle to break through the strongest mine-field defences ever organized in Africa, he lost many more tanks than his opponent, but fought with the certainty that a far larger proportion of the cripples would be recovered. Above all, he never let down his guard. At Medenine he was so well prepared that Rommel's last tank attack was a disastrous rout.

For the British the campaigns in South-East Asia involved learning painful lessons in jungle and forest warfare for which the Japanese had trained before entering the war. Nor could British or Indian troops ever emulate all the devices with the aid of which the Japanese won so many crushing victories in the first phase. When the baseball player Babe Ruth was asked to explain his methods he replied: 'Hitting 'em where they ain't.' ('Em' were the balls and 'they' the fielders.) The Japanese were expert in this practice, and they used it not only when on the offensive but also when on the defensive in the Arakan. They would walk quietly into a position undefended but in their hands blocking British communications, fortify it, and prepare to hold it to the last. The reason the British could not imitate them often was that the troops could not subsist on the austere régime, to say nothing of the dirt and squalor, of such isolated posts. Yet by jungle training, both on training grounds and in contact with the enemy, the British finally made themselves at home and with superior equipment and numbers inflicted on the Japanese one of the most thorough defeats of the war.

Many of the struggles for the Pacific Islands represented war carried to its theoretical extreme. The refusal of the Japanese soldier to surrender led to battles of extermination. The American troops mainly responsible for the operations until large armies were required in the Philippines were the Marines, who possessed an aptitude for them. In no operations of the war was the combination of infantry, naval artillery, and aircraft from carriers or airfields closer or more effective. On the smaller islands especially, the fighting was primitive in that it depended to so great an extent upon the skill in minor tactics of the most junior officers and even individual soldiers. It was primitive also in the sense that though the weapons employed were modern, those used by the troops were necessarily light; in fact, it came down largely to hand weapons. There was a remarkable contrast between the fighting ashore with the weapons carried on the man, and the support from the huge shells of Japanese battleships off Guadalcanal or from American in later combined operations.

The campaign in the Philippines was on so great a scale that, after the landings, it assumed a normal complexion, except that the Japanese made a supreme effort to isolate the army by defeating the naval forces and destroying the supply ships. The next objective, Okinawa, required as the final bomber base, was far more bitterly contested. Its capture took just short of twelve weeks, though it was only about 70 miles long and very narrow, and cost the Americans 39,000 casualties. This is a campaign which aroused strong criticism and allegations in the United States that clumsy tactics caused unnecessary loss. The deepest tragedy of Okinawa was, however, that the stoutness of the Japanese resistance was a big factor in the American decision to drop the atomic bombs.

The last theatre at which we glance is North-West Europe. Whereas, however, this is of high interest from the strategic point of view, it is much less so from the tactical. Sea and air power in combination put the allies ashore. Sea power gave them valuable support within the range of the guns and afterwards protected their communications. Thereafter the battlefields were dominated by the combination of the tank and the fighter-bomber. In the land weapon the British and Americans were in considerable superiority; in that of the air they met no serious resistance.

Sparkling tactical feats were performed. In the break-out from the bridgehead reconnaissance was on several occasions bold and skilful and reports were in some instances transmitted by wireless from within the German lines. The mating of armour and motorized infantry in 'combat groups' worked well, but might not have done so but for the superiority in armoured strength because the infantry was road-bound to an undue degree and the armoured element in the division probably too small in proportion to the total strength of the division.[4] In the final stages certain British, Canadian, American, and French Armoured divisions were handled with great dash and skill. On the German side the Ardennes offensive, while strategically a disaster, was tactically brilliant in the Fifth Panzer Army. Individual allied squadrons, even single tanks, manœuvred well to tackle the more heavily-gunned German tanks, which were capable of knocking them out at nearly twice the range. On the whole, however, it was a slogging match: the attack depended rather on quick shooting and air support than on manœuvre; the defence on the deadly 88-mm. gun.

To sum up, even before the appearance of the atomic bomb, to say nothing of the later tactical atomic weapons, to those professionally interested in tactics, whether as fighting men or theorists, there seemed to

[4] Hart, *The Tanks*, Vol. ii, p. 456.

be much to revise. In some cases former lessons seemed to have been forgotten or dismissed as inappropriate to the conditions of North-West Europe. In others new ideas and devices appeared to be called for. Is it not possible to apply the tactics of the North African desert, perhaps not entirely but to a greater extent, to typically western and central European country? It cannot be done unless infantry, and especially that which is a component of armoured formations, can be given greater freedom of cross-country mobility. Only tracked armoured vehicles can provide this. They would render feasible open and flexible manœuvre in attack, afford a measure of protection against tactical atomic weapons, and at the same time favour speedy regrouping for defence.

Chapter Eleven

NUCLEAR WARFARE

MANY people, in all probability the majority, believe that there is no point in studying nuclear warfare in terms of strategy and tactics or, in other words, of the art of war. How can there be an art, they demand, in mass destruction, and in the case of small and easily accessible countries, virtual obliteration? Yet this kind of warfare is susceptible of analysis, and by reducing it to first principles we discover that it involves problems on which there are differences of opinion. Even the assailant has to make decisions about his method of attack. And ever since the bomb was dropped on Hiroshima governments and their military and scientific advisers have been thrashing out the subject. It may be that their work will prove fruitless, that the thing is already or will become so colossal as to render policy needless in attack and useless in defence because there will be such a superfluity of power as to swamp all else. This, however, ought not to be assumed without examination.

What would be the object of a full-scale nuclear attack, let us say by Soviet Russia on the United States? To put the country out of action by a single blow or quick succession of blows. But the attack would not be directed against *everything* in the United States in the hope that the circles of destruction created by individual bombs would intersect each other in such a way as to cover the whole country. Therefore, although nuclear attack is certainly the least selective of all forms of warfare, there would be some sort of selection. When we get that we get strategy.

The first question the Russian planner would ask himself might be whether the assault should be delivered against the great cities, the air forces, or both. He would then decide that two objectives might well be one too many or at all events that attacks ought not to be delivered in equal strength and that one or other should have priority; if he considered the secondary one it would of course be because his means were ample. He would find little difficulty in establishing the priority. He would be clear in his mind that the defence policy of the United States was based upon the deterrent prospect of immediate and heavy retaliation and that American planning would break down unless this retaliation was assured. If he put the United States Air Force out of action the cities would lie at his mercy. Therefore he would make the United States Air Force his primary objective, not only the long-range bombers which were there to carry bombs against his own country but the fighter squadrons with which he would immediately afterwards have to reckon. He might still be able to afford the means to attack a secondary objective, perhaps to destroy the political capital, Washington, the business capital, New York, and, possibly something more.

Before he got thus far, however, he would have to consider the bases outside the United States from which reprisals would be directed. Unless he provided also for their destruction or neutralization, the reprisals would be devastating. Great Britain, the Federal Republic of Germany, and certain Far Eastern bases would in particular be scheduled for attack. Special attention would be paid to fleets, above all the American fleets in the Mediterranean and Western Pacific, possessing long-range nuclear bombers in their carriers, and submarines equipped with guided missiles. It will appear that all this—and there is much more—calls for deep consideration and that revision is likely to be unending. Similar problems will confront the planner of the counter-offensive. Yet there is one important difference: the attacker may benefit from a measure of surprise—the extent is disputed but it seems generally agreed that he may hope for some. The defender can count on none. If the attack is automatically followed by the counter-attack, the latter can contain no element of surprise. Nor is it likely to find the enemy's air bases very profitable targets because attack on them will be treated as a certainty.

It must be granted that the defender's hand is a weak one. His one strong card is his prepared reprisal, and the main strength of this lies in its not being used. Those given to dialectic take pleasure in telling us that, if it is used, the conclusion must be that it has failed before being put into use. We may disregard this over-subtlety because it would in fact be most important to get the counter-offensive working, and at maximum strength. The United States is not going to be blotted out in a few hours: to suggest that it is is to indulge in the hyperbole so often created by panic and despair. The extent of the destruction of life and property and the period required for a return to relative normality is hard to determine and the estimates have varied enormously. This is not to conclude that efforts to improve the situation will not be made or that they are foredoomed to complete failure.

The first requirement of the defence is an efficient warning system. This is a field upon which both N.A.T.O. and its most powerful members have concentrated. The radar warning system is closely linked with an immense signals and communication network. Then there are the weapons of interception in the form of guided missiles: air to air, ground to air, and ground to ground. The guiding may be done by remote control from the ground, from a ship or even from an aircraft. For short ranges the missile can be fitted with its own directing devices. In one case it has been revealed that the missile detects a hostile bomber by the heat of its engines and can then automatically alter course to bring about a collision. Needless to say, more subtle devices still are the objects of continual research, but the outsider is likely to know little about their relative success or failure, or even about the defects and margins of error of those already in production.

Lastly, we come to the Achilles heel, civil defence. It is down at the bottom of the list of preparations, in most countries derisory if measured in cash. The main causes of this are two. In the first place, advance measures which are theoretically possible and would certainly result in the saving of millions of lives in a nuclear war would require colossal sums. For example, suppose that a government decided to establish camps in which a fifth of the population could be housed in huts, with water laid on and protection against radio-active 'fall-out' provided. Apart from the cost in cash, the demands on labour and materials would probably be so vast as to disrupt the national economy. The camps would then need a small army of guardians to preserve them from fire and theft. Yet if this were not done in advance, evacuation on the above scale might be impossible. The second handicap is the widespread belief that the destructive power of nuclear weapons is so tremendous that all measures of civil defence are useless. Sometimes the policy of doing nothing is advocated by those who have abandoned themselves to despair; sometimes it is due to sulkiness because governments will not agree to the proposal of the objectors, to strip away all measures of defence and confront the peril in naked virtue. The difficulties are peculiarly heavy in Britain because it is small, thickly populated, highly industrialized, and physically not in general suitable for the provision of under-ground shelter. In countries which are—for example, Norway, a member of N.A.T.O., and Switzerland, a neutral—a considerable amount of work of this sort had been done by the year 1959.

In the United States a document was produced in 1958 by an organization sponsored by the Government, the RAND Corporation. It was entitled *Report on a Study of Non-Military Defense*. The work was done by some twenty experts in various fields. The tentative conclusions are worthy of mention, not because they can readily be checked but because the RAND Corporation has knowledge, skill, the technique of analysis, and objectivity. They are better worth consideration than the intuitions and preconceptions so often aired.

These conclusions have been called tentative. They are where figures are concerned, but they are confident in denying the inevitability of 'mutual annihilation'. Their background is the United States. The essential conclusion is that attainable measures of defence can preserve society. The team could take only relatively short views because the threat changes. They concluded that an expenditure of a billion dollars[1] or less could, during the early 'sixties of this century, be counted on 'with high confidence' to protect half the population and an additional quarter 'with medium confidence'. They also concluded that such a programme of defence could be undertaken in stages, that each stage would pay its way, that none would create irrevocable commitments, and that each would prove an appropriate step towards meeting the conditions likely to prevail in a period beyond the immediate purview of the planners.

The subject does not readily lend itself to compression, because the report itself, though many times larger than the space that can here be given to it, is already compressed. It can only be added that the problems of radio-activity are taken into account, that the aid which

[1] It must be remembered that an American billion is a thousand millions. A billion dollars thus represents at the exchange rate of 1959 about £350,000,000.

military defence can give to civil—or, as Americans call it, 'non-military' defence—is considered, and that an interesting study of the possible effects of such preparations on American foreign policy is included. The report is in full agreement with the view expressed earlier in this chapter—a view actually reached before studying the RAND document—that it is 'important to get the counter-offensive working', and that the measures prepared to serve as a deterrent are not in fact useless because they have failed to deter.

Unhappily, from the Briton's point of view, defence wears a less promising—or more depressing—aspect for his own country than for the United States. Britain would have less warning and less room. It would also seem that, if the long-range missile becomes more and more the predominant means of delivering a nuclear weapon, as appears likely, the displacement of the aircraft in that role will be to the disadvantage of the defence. In civil defence pure and simple it may not make a great difference. A bomb is a bomb, however it arrives, and strictly civil measures of defence such as shelter from blast, protection from radio-activity, dispersal, assistance, supplies of food and water, and rehabilitation, are the same. On the other hand, the aid given to civil by military defence is unlikely to be as efficacious against long-range missiles as against bombs carried by aircraft. As these words are written at all events, they are written with the certainty that military defence is in this position now.

This is not the last word on the subject of guided

missiles. Science, all the combination of sciences connected with this repellent subject, is working at a great pace. Yet science is also being applied to methods of attack, in which its path is easier. It can not only make the weapons of attack more deadly but also increase their effect by various devices for interrupting or confusing the apparatus of warning and the communications system. For the outsider, optimism about the possibility of countering missile weapons would be misplaced.

Just as a great deal of opinion derides the study of warfare waged by means of the megaton bomb, so it refuses to discuss anything but limited or 'conventional' warfare in terms of armies and fleets. It writes off the subject. Yet Soviet Russia would not have maintained until the year 1959 about 140 active divisions, about half of them armoured, 65 to 70 in the European theatre *in the first instance*, and a vast tactical air force organized in air armies, if her rulers and their professional advisers had not considered them useful.[2]

It is true that in January 1960 the all-powerful Russian leader suddenly announced that the armed forces of the Soviet Union had been reduced by 1,200,000, that is, from 3,623,000 to 2,423,000, and claimed this action as a measure of disarmament which should be imitated by the United States and the United Kingdom. In point of fact, Russia was not showing the way but imitating action taken in the United States in 1955 and in the United Kingdom in 1957, in the reduction of conventional forces. It would be absurd to

[2] *The Fifteen Nations*, No. 9/10, pp. 54–56.

describe the reduction as sinister, but it might have the sinister implication that the only war worth preparing for was a full-scale nuclear war. And it should be noted that this step was announced within a few days of the first official hint heard in Britain that the country's policy might have been tethered too tightly to the nuclear deterrent and that more attention should be paid to preparation and equipment for conventional warfare in future.

At the same time it must be realized that a strength of 2,423,000 first-line or active troops still represents vast forces of land, sea, and air, backed by a colossal trained reserve. It may well be that the reduction was based upon the belief that a stronger labour force was necessary to the Soviet Union. It would be wrong, on this evidence alone, to jump to the conclusion that the Russian Government did not desire general measures of disarmament, and equally wrong to assume that she had left herself incapable of waging conventional war. It remains worth while to study sea and land warfare, even if only to summarize features which create speculation and argument.

In nuclear warfare the heaviest weapons are not the most suitable for employment against land armies. They are essentially long-range weapons. The aggressor who uses them does not want their explosions to be made too close to his own land forces, which might indeed be hung up by them and find it impossible to advance. For this reason what are called 'tactical atomic weapons' have been introduced. When they were first heard of they were thought popularly to be very confined in their effects, but most intelligent people now know that this is an error and that they are capable of bringing about enormous destruction over a wide area. In this country a group of intelligent critics considered the possibility that, by general consent, in a war fought for issues falling short of the strongest the belligerents might confine themselves to tactical atomic weapons. It is here maintained that the chances are small. On the other hand, field armies might fight each other with the smaller weapons only. They could not keep it up for long if their home countries and bases were put out of action by the greater weapons, over their heads, but at least the forces of one side might remain in being. Foresight, training, and preparation can contribute to this result.

Tactics and the organization on which they are based would have to be revised. Indeed, steps to this end began in the late 'fifties. The first obvious action is to reduce the size of formations or organize them so that they can be split and can operate equally well in smaller units, which the old-fashioned type of division could not. Lines of communication should be multiplied because those dependent on main roads and railways and major ports cannot be relied on. This calls for transport suitable for use on third-rate roads or even lanes and indeed for vehicles able to move across country on reasonably favourable ground. It calls for movement under the veil of darkness whenever possible, which in its turn demands a high standard of training. It requires protection and incessant digging to provide it at every move. In fact, the last is about the most vital consideration, and some of the studies made seem to have reached over-optimistic conclusions. It is only on suitable ground, such as that of most of Western Germany where so many experiments have been made, that men can constantly and swiftly dig themselves in with their immediate needs, to say nothing of their vehicles. Moreover, the period for which they can maintain a state of efficiency while living this sort of life must be limited.

Night actions are of course even more difficult than night tactical movements, and they almost always involve some confusion. Yet they have the advantage that even if they fall short of full success or fail altogether the penalty will in most cases be lighter than by day. And it is easy to see, though at first glance paradoxical, that, when facing tactical atomic weapons, it is safer to be in close contact with the enemy than a considerable distance away. In fact, if the enemy wants to use these weapons he will have to break contact first. The Japanese proved in the Second World War how demoralizing night attack might be. Since the appearance of tactical atomic weapons it may be more effective still.

What has caused most dispute in discussions about atomic warfare at sea is the role of carriers. 'Their days are, no doubt, numbered and the time will come when there will be a better way of doing the job than packing a lot of ordinary aircraft into one steel-hull that would obviously be the first target for attack', writes a distinguished Marshal of the R.A.F.[3] On the

[3] Slessor, *Strategy for the West*, p. 93.

other hand, the United States is at the time of writing maintaining a great number of enormously expensive carriers and employing them even in the land-locked Mediterranean. The critical airman is assuredly right in his statement that this is the most costly way to base aircraft. On the other hand, the believers in carriers point out that they are highly mobile bases. They make one vivid statement which is perfectly true but not conclusive: that a carrier, the position of which has been reported at nightfall, may be well over 200 miles away by daylight or anywhere in a circle with an area of over 120,000 square miles.[4] This is based on the assumption that the position has been discovered immediately before the ship is hidden by darkness and that there is no time for an attack. In fact, some form of guided missile might be launched against it in a matter of minutes. It slurs the fact that the ship is highly vulnerable in daylight, even though its concentrated weapons of defence are extremely powerful. Again, if the switch from aircraft to guided missile takes place, defensive powers are likely to be lessened. It would, however, appear that, in the conditions of 1959 the mobility of the carrier provides opportunities for sudden blows, and that though these would not have anything like the force of those delivered from airfields or by guided missiles, carriers are less easy to put out of action before the strike is delivered. In any case, carriers have other purposes. They are invaluable in 'conventional' warfare, though they need not for that purpose attain the

[4] $\pi \times$ sq. of radius $= 3.1416 \times 40,000$ sq. miles.

size of the monsters forming part of the United States Navy.

The other offensive craft of the modern navy is the submarine. It has acquired by technical improvements the ability to remain for very long periods below the surface and at the same time a considerably increased submerged speed. Soviet Russia had built by the end of 1958, according to British estimates, at least 500 of these boats, of which 'a large percentage are of the most modern type' and possess a radius of action 'adapted to the high seas'.[5] This is the major development in Russian strategy since the Second World War. Its chief aim is considered to be that of cutting off Europe from the New World and rendering impossible access of American naval forces either to European waters or to those of Asia. (It may be noted that if this interpretation is correct—and it can scarcely be wrong—the Soviet strategists do not believe that a full-scale war would necessarily end in a few days.) The submarines could, however, undertake other missions. Norwegian reports indicate that trials with guided missiles fired from these boats have been going on since 1956 in the Barents Sea. One handicap which faces Russian naval forces is that the Baltic and the Black Sea are enclosed waters where separate fleets under independent commands must be maintained, and that the Arctic and Pacific are both separated from them, though the Baltic has a connexion with the Arctic by canal. This situation could be bettered by a quick conquest of Scandinavia.

[5] *The Fifteen Nations*, No. 9/10, p. 47.

Speed is obviously a factor of importance in nuclear war at sea. The latest Russian destroyers built for the high seas are credited with a speed of 38 knots. It will, however, be a long time before fleets of atomic powered vessels take the stage, and until then oil will retain its place. Ships sailing at maximum speed expend a higher proportion of their oil to cover the same distance than if they move at a slower speed, which is known as 'economical'. A certain number of atomic-powered submarines had appeared by 1959, and oil-burning boats have been refuelled by others acting as oilers as long ago as the Second World War. Speed not only gives a ship a better chance of escaping pursuit but improves the chance of evading it with the aid of the weather. A fast ship can gain the protection of low cloud in a shorter time than a slow one.

On the whole, navies would seem to have prospects of remaining in action in nuclear warfare as long as land armies, if not longer. Both have to face the fact that, assuming a fair proportion to have escaped the consequences of direct attack, neither can hope to remain an effective fighting force if their bases are put out of action. Navies and single ships can, however, change their bases quicker than land forces and use new bases much farther away from the old ones. Food is always food and fuel oil always fuel oil. Ammunition for British naval guns might be stored in the British West Indies, in Canada, or for that matter in the United States if the risk of war became grave.

This subject is in some quarters regarded as not merely impossible to handle with profit but even as one which reflects disgrace upon the student who handles it. The calm and inquiring mind ought not to submit to prejudice of the latter sort. The generally speculative comments set down here are not attempts to belittle the immensity of the threat aimed at millions of human beings by nuclear weapons. They are not a denial of the certainty that science hides still more horrible giants in its womb. If these comments are unsatisfactory, the fault may lie partly in failures in the analysis attempted; but it seems fair to claim that the heaviest handicap has been the extent to which the speculation mentioned enters into the examination. This would probably apply also to more instructed studies, carried out by those in possession of more precise information.

The present threat is far more deadly than any inherent in former methods of attack, but preparation to meet it is still not without profit. Forethought is seldom wasted and is most unlikely to be wholly wasted here. All human lives and most of the work of men's hands that can be saved are worth saving. It is a national duty to make efforts to save them. Despair is not a policy.

The object of every wise nation should be to find a means of ending the menace; but how is the cordage of distrust which throttles the states of the opposed camps to be cut? In the latter part of the year 1959 and early in 1960 the Soviet leader seemed to be actuated by a genuine desire for international disarmament.

He also showed signs of conviction that a nuclear war would be as disastrous for Russia as for her foes and a consequent urge to avoid one. The extreme popular optimism which arose in the free world—despite the caution of those who spoke for its governments —met with a sickening shock when on 17 May he suddenly refused to take part in the long-awaited 'Summit' conference. This did not so much fail as fail to start.

The above is the last historical event which can be mentioned here. It is set down chiefly as proof of how difficult negotiations with Communist Russia had become. The approach of those who sought it may be likened to that of a man walking up to the mouth of a cave to bargain with another man sheltered in its darkness. The former is plainly visible, and his plans and aspirations are almost as clear as his person. The latter can scarcely be discerned, and his motives are completely shrouded. After the break-down the organs of opinion found themselves at a loss. The explanation, they suggested, might be pure spleen created by American clumsiness. On the other hand, the dictator might not be dictating any longer; a new force might have appeared in Russia and caused a shift to a more aggressive policy. China might have provided the stimulant—and so on. But the examination must end.

We should not need exhortation to make up our minds what this involves. That it calls for further efforts to reach a settlement goes without saying. Meanwhile objective study of doctrine, armament, and training in all forms of defence remain as vital as ever. It must include appreciations of how far defences and the economy can be kept working if all endeavours to hold off the catastrophe of nuclear war should fail.

Chapter Twelve

A LOOK BACK

THIS study has been cast in historical form, though an effort has also been made to throw light upon 'the act of war as a whole'. The final review will be of the same character. In the period of a century and a half from the rise of the young Bonaparte to the Hiroshima bomb of 1945 belligerents often enough found themselves unprepared in mind or equipment for the type of war which came about. Sometimes this applied to one side only, but there were cases—in the First World War, for example—where it applied to both. Yet between one war and the next certain guiding lights were never extinguished. There were means of forecasting what would happen, though they were not properly utilized, in most cases because prejudices and preconceptions in even the best minds prevented logical and objective analysis. *Someone* always foresaw the future accurately.

We now face a greater revolution than any in the history of warfare. Atomic energy is far more revolutionary than firearms, the submarine, the tank, or even the aircraft. The two first-named were not properly speaking revolutionary at all, since the word implies swift as well as drastic change. The bow survived for a century beside the arquebus and the musket. The submarine had formed part of the navies of several

powers for some fifteen years before it began to play a
vital part in war. The tank was in a sense a revival, a
war chariot brought up to date, but it developed slowly.
The aircraft certainly altered war completely, but far
from 'revolutionizing' it, exercised only a minor effect
upon the First World War. Though it proved difficult
to foresee the future of these tools of war both when
they were novelties and at vital stages of their development, and of others such as the marine engine, the
locomotive, the breach-loading rifle, the machine gun,
and the internal combustion engine, they were
more calculable than the weapons of nuclear fission.
None of their predecessors could produce destruction
on so vast a scale. This wholesale, all-pervading,
annihilating quality divides nuclear weapons from all
others. It renders far more difficult the task of analysing
their characteristics as applied to war.

As stated in the previous chapter, many people believe
that there is nothing left to analyse. They hold that
the absolute has been reached. They foresee, in the
event of a nuclear war, the possible destruction of
mankind and the virtually certain destruction of
civilization. In the few pages allotted to the subject
here this view has not been taken. Yet the reservations
advanced have been written against a background of
further horror, since it is only too certain that the last
discovery has not been made and that fresh destructive
power will be attained. It does not appear to the writer
that, brief and slight as has been the study of nuclear
fission as a means of waging war, there is anything more
that can usefully be added to it—at all events by him.

So the winding-up will be concerned with the century and a half preceding the event which occurred at Hiroshima on 6 August 1945.

Leaving 'the bomb' out of account, it may be said that strategy is marked by a number of unchanging characteristics. It does change in scale, though Marlborough's march to the Danube in 1704 was on a scale to which there are not many parallels in the period under review. Certain ideas have been so often illustrated or have struck the minds of observers so forcibly that they have been given the status of principles. Thus we say that, wherever the possibility of surprise arises, it should be brought about, because surprise adds enormously to the force of the blow delivered and many attacks which will succeed with its aid will be defeated if the enemy discovers what is afoot and has time to alter his dispositions in order to deal with it. We also distinguish between strategic and tactical surprise. The first is founded on secret movements which place the enemy at a disadvantage, for example, by bringing superior strength to bear on a weak part of his array, without giving him time to reinforce it. The second is the actual launching of an attack when or where the enemy does not expect one. We also associate surprise with concentration of strength, as mentioned in the introductory chapter, because the two support each other. The skilled strategist will, however, nowadays commonly postpone his concentration, not only to facilitate surprise but because he wants to postpone his plan of operations until he is thoroughly acquainted with the enemy's dispositions or to take advantage of any slip the latter may make. A well-balanced and well-articulated dispersion seeking information through feelers, after the manner of insects and crustacea furnished with antennae, is probably the ideal preliminary disposition of an army, though it may not be suitable to every occasion. This does not conflict with the sound adage: 'Keep detachments as small as possible,' which might run conversely: 'Put the maximum possible strength into the main attack.'

Again, though the unintellectual officer may be impatient of discussion about the relation of the army and its line or lines of communication, a great deal that the theorists say on the subject is bottled common sense. The base is the point or line from which operations start; the line of communications is the route of supplies to the army.[1] There is no difficulty in seeing, when the point is explained, that danger exists in fighting parallel to the line of communication, or in military terms 'forming front to a flank'. When one side does this and the other does not, then the former, if defeated, may be driven over and off its communications; if the latter is defeated it can fall back along them and maintain contact with its base. The first situation may be a disaster, the second no more than a setback.

In the same way debate about the pros and cons of 'exterior' and 'interior' lines, at first sight daunting or even repellent, is concerned with simple ideas. The terms are, however, somewhat complicated because they are used in slightly different senses. Germany

---

[1] Falls, *Ordeal by Battle*, p. 72. The problems of this kind are treated more fully here.

fought both world wars on interior lines because she held a central position—crossed by first-class railways —from which she could concentrate strength against her western and eastern foes in turn. The advantage is the possibility of putting one foe out of action by such means, and this, with the aid of the Russian revolution, is what Germany did in the First World War. The disadvantage is the possibility of being squeezed from both sides, and this is what happened in the Second World War. The second situation in which the terms are used is one where, to take the simplest example, one side is concentrated in face of two separated forces, each half its own strength. The former is said to be on interior lines, the latter on exterior lines. It will obviously pay the concentrated force if it can throw, let us say, three-quarters of its strength by surprise against one of the divided forces—a superiority of 50 per cent—while watching or holding off the other with one quarter. The concept is indeed simple. All lies in the execution.

Since the Franco-Prussian War, armies have constantly tried to avoid purely frontal attacks in order to avoid facing the full weight of the new fire-power. Their effort then aims at reaching one of the enemy's flanks and rolling it up. Why not, the tiro may ask, turn and roll up both flanks? Well, if you do, this may be the quietus. It was when Hannibal brought it off at Cannae. Yet it presupposes very great numerical or qualitative superiority, and if the strength is inadequate the enemy may react by breaking your centre. One flank is usually all that is within your means, but nature may provide an anvil to your hammer, the sea for example.

Clausewitz has caused grinding of teeth, ever since *Vom Kriege* was published, by one brief sentence: 'defence is the stronger form of war'. This has been generally denied, sometimes derided, rarely understood. Its truth is in fact elementary. Why does the commander with a force half the size of the enemy's, or who has suffered a defeat already, or who awaits reinforcements, or who expects another army of his country to draw off some of the enemy's strength in the near future, or who wants to dictate the battlefield and sees no other way of doing it—why does a general in any of these situations commonly stand on the defensive? Because he thinks it improves his chances. Great commanders have been doing it for centuries, and it is impossible to believe that they have generally been wrong. In the words of a famous writer on war, General von der Goltz, 'the fundamental idea behind the strategic defensive is to remedy an unfavourable situation by husbanding our own forces while those of the enemy are more rapidly consumed in the attack'. Quite so, but work it out as the logician Clausewitz did. If the commander who stands on the defensive is right in thinking that this improves his chance and that he should at all events wear out the enemy faster than his force is worn out, *then the defensive must be something added to his fighting strength.* In other words, 'defence is the stronger form of war'.

Clausewitz did not say that it was the most desirable form of war; he considered indeed that it ought to be given up at the earliest opportunity. It does not prove the stronger form in all circumstances. On the contrary, the great victorious offensives which form the essence of the history of war are most often far less costly to attacker than to defender. At its best the defensive postpones a decision more often than it brings one about. Yet this saying of Clausewitz presents the commander on the offensive with a valuable hint. Provided the enemy will oblige him by launching a counterstroke which he has a good prospect of defeating, it may well pay him to fight a purely defensive battle in the midst of his offensive campaign. Montgomery did so at Medenine in March 1943. 'Perhaps this might prove another Alam Halfa, a defensive battle which would help the offensive one which followed.'[2] It did. Without the victory of Medenine the Mareth Line might not have been breached. We must, however, bear in mind that the relative strength of attack and defence is not constant. It fluctuates with the changes in weapons and methods of fighting. In western Europe the defensive was stronger in the First World War than in the Second, and stronger in some phases of the latter than in others. As a rule, much blood and sweat are expended before leaders discover which is in the ascendant.

In the same way, the tactics of land warfare have developed with changes in weapons, but have generally lagged behind them. Everyone is familiar with the jibe that the next war is always faced with the ideas of the last. Soldiers' minds often fail to keep up with the

[2] Montgomery, *The Memoirs of Field-Marshal Montgomery*, p. 158.

advance of weapons, though completely familiar with
them. The Japanese approached modern war objectively just because it was new to them and they had
developed the use of European weapons with extraordinary speed. Yet when they faced Russia in 1904
they found that their tactics were far too expensive,
even though they never suffered defeat in battle. Before
the end in Manchuria they had modified them. They
made much more use of cover in attack and were
content to lessen the speed of their advance in order to
make this possible.[3] Yet this is not always the case.
Those who are never happy except when deriding the
soldier for being behind the times carry their criticism
too far. When the Japanese Army entered Malaya in
the Second World War it had already perfected the arts
of jungle, forest, and plantation warfare. And no one
can maintain that leaders of armoured forces such as
the German Heinz Guderian, Hermann Hoth, and
Erwin Rommel were either slow-minded or reactionary.
They had foreseen the devastating possibilities of the
tank when boldly and skilfully handled, swerving
round centres of resistance and penetrating weak places
at top speed. We may also say that the handling of
troops in retreat in 1940 by Brooke and his lieutenants
Alexander, Montgomery, and Franklyn showed that
they realized the difference between this war and the
last, in which all four of them had served.

One of the handicaps to 'keeping up with the Joneses'
in warfare is that men of action are seldom seers and
seers even less often men of action. The seer may be

[3] Fuller, *The Decisive Battles*, Vol. iii, p. 166.

invaluable to soldiers, but his influence is unlikely to be great unless he is also an enterprising soldier endowed with a personality and the gift of leadership. The professional is generally scornful about the 'armchair strategist', though lawyers who have triumphed at the bar and won high reputations on the bench have often owed much of their success to the teaching of academic lawyers who have never had a client. It is also the case that there have been magnificent soldiers who started as pure amateurs or, as the Cardinal de Retz puts it, were 'born as captains'. Among them were Condé, Spinola, Cromwell, and in the twentieth century, Pilsudski. There is indeed a form of arm-chair strategy which merits contempt: that which makes pronouncement from the map alone, without weighing the factors of communications, supply, weapons, training. You can learn 'the business of war' only by service in armed forces, though it can be done without ever hearing a shot fired in anger. On the other hand, you can learn the ideas of war—whether or not they are called 'principles'—in the study. Neither is a mystery. When it comes to command, however, character is necessary. The conventional soldiers who are always talking about character may be bores, but it is a prerequisite of leadership.

The problems of supply depend upon training and experience even more than the art of fighting. Oddly enough, success in solving them has had a hampering effect on armies, particularly the United States Army which supplies its soldiers on the most luxurious scale enjoyed by any armed forces. Confectionery, ices and

iced drinks, columns of trucks to carry men a couple
of miles to baths, 'comics' for light reading, mobile
cinematographs—none of these comforts are in principle wasteful; but when they are piled up they
create little armies and employ too much man-power.
In adversity and retreat they become a positive menace
by cluttering roads, as occurred in the Korean War.
One of the problems faced by wealthy and lavish
nations—and one which has at last been recognized
as such—is, not to improve the amenities of troops
on campaign by increasing their transport, but to
render them more mobile and present fewer targets on
the roads by cutting out superfluities.

One handicap created by excessive transport hardly
existed in the First World War, at least on the Western
Front, but became obvious in the Second. It is the
increased fluidity of warfare. The speed of a modern
advance commonly leaves uncleared and even unex-
plored vast areas of country in which bodies of hostile
troops have been outstripped in their retreat. These
men, though 'perhaps only seeking to capture food,
vehicles, and fuel in the hope of escape, may prove
highly dangerous to administrative services. Again,
forces may be deliberately organized for deep raids . . .
and guerrilla bands may operate far to the rear'. So
the movement of convoys becomes a tactical as well as
a military operation and supply services must be armed
and trained to defend themselves.[4] The fewer the
'soft-skinned' vehicles, the less onerous will be the task.
And no commander would welcome having to provide

[4] Falls, *A Hundred Years of War*, p. 257.

armoured cars to escort out of danger a soft-skinned prima donna who had been singing to the troops.

Yet supply can never be economical in the civilian sense because it is faced with so many accidents and because the reserves must be so large. Sudden demands for the movement of goods exceeding the normal capacity of available transport have to be foreseen. The proportion of goods such as ammunition and fuel which is kept on wheels appears extravagant and sometimes is so, but those who thus withdraw vehicles temporarily from service want to be on the safe side. They are inspired both by a sense of duty and by an understandable fear than an hour's delay in the delivery of these two staples of war will bring down censure upon them and that no explanations will be accepted. Who that has served in war fails to recall the hoarding and 'scrounging' of the quartermaster and how greatly he was appreciated if he could always produce what was wanted—and no questions asked?

The improvement in the speed and reliability of mechanical transport tended to make the Second World War to a lesser extent than the First a 'railway war'. Those who believe that railways sank into insignificance, however, are hopelessly ignorant of the administrative background. Railways were indispensable. They were always restored as quickly as possible after being put out of action. The Germans expended immense energy and man-power in converting the broad-gauge Russian railways to European standard-gauge. What did happen was that a campaign could be maintained by road in the later war up to about eight times as great a distance from ports or railheads as had been possible in the earlier, and for a considerable period. Air supply has made rapid strides since the Second World War. It can carry out virtually any task demanded of it—provided that the aircraft can be protected.

Only two powers in the world now possess vast naval fleets. They are the United States and Russia, and the latter's is almost entirely a cruiser and submarine fleet. Since a fleet battle between these countries could normally be fought only when they were committed to a full-scale war against each other; since a full-scale war would inevitably become a nuclear war; and since a fleet battle like Jutland or even Leyte would be impossible in a nuclear war, there will never be another such battle. As for the tasks which are likely to be called for from naval forces in nuclear warfare, is is to be doubted whether any but those of the United States and Russia are capable of performing them. Britain, within the memory of those who are not yet old the undisputed queen of the seas, could never have hoped to maintain her naval strength above or near the level of that of the United States, given her losses in two wars and her lavish social policy. She might none the less have kept together the nucleus of a navy capable of playing a creditable and effective part against submarines in war. She appears to have done nothing of the kind. Indeed, when questions on the subject are asked in high places the answer is generally to the effect that we are members of an alliance and that the United States will take care of the Atlantic in war. This is a humiliating situation, but that might be disregarded if the hope were well based. One may suppose that the United States would indeed do her best to maintain the Atlantic sea routes, but she would have her hands full and it is only to be expected that she would concentrate first on that part of the programme which most affected her own direct interests.

Conventional warfare, on the other hand, is not so costly, and states of the second order like Britain and France can afford to make themselves proficient in it. Here the call today is for speed in reaching the scene and clearing up the trouble. In these times when 'cold' wars may give way to 'hot' between sunset and sunrise, a day's needless delay may lead to the overthrow of a friendly state. The combination of aircraft carrier, landing craft and, where a forced landing is called for, a vanguard of parachute troops, appears the ideal 'task force' for the smaller enterprises. However, conventional warfare can be called cheap either in preparation or operation only in relation to nuclear warfare. The small and brief action at Port Said in 1956 cost millions. It also revealed deficiencies in equipment which might prove serious in an affair similar in character but in which resistance was stouter and better organized. For example, helicopters could not be used as they were by the British at Port Said, to land a commando on a beach on which only a narrow footing had been obtained, in face of defenders capable of serious resistance. The reader—whether in London or in Moscow—at home in military organization must have commented at sight of the first accounts of the landing: 'shortage of means due to shortage of funds'. In the same way it may be said with confidence that the first reaction of the British Admiralty was the desirability of increasing the number of its Marine Commandos, as representing the most useful type of all-round soldiers that could be conceived.

In fact, the main problem facing Britain, the second power in the free world and bearing the greatest share of small-scale obligations, is how to divide her expenditure between nuclear and 'conventional' warfare. Probably the main weight of opinion among military commentators was that by 1959 the former was getting more than its share of the cake. They argued that the Communist camp, directed by Soviet Russia, would be enabled to get all it wanted by steady penetration, never taking more than a short step forward at any time but never stopping the pressure, so that the preparations for nuclear warfare in the Western camp would prove useless. There is indeed much to be said for this view. In the year which is that of the final survey, 1959, it was clear that the immediate danger came from strictly controlled and limited thrusts in Asia, combined with highly organized propaganda. Only twice had a major operation been attempted, in Korea and the former French Indo-China, in the first defeated, in the second victorious. The others, either threats later allowed to die down, successful anti-Communist interventions or threats concerned with the future, affected the Kars-Ardahan region of north-east Turkey, northern Persia, the Formosa

Strait, Lebanon, Jordan, the Aden littoral, Tibet, Laos, and Sikkim and Bhutan on the flank of the Himalayas. The reason for this long list of Far Eastern and Middle Eastern outrages or threats of them was in great part the setting up of N.A.T.O., which heavily checked Communism in Europe and dealt it the shrewdest blow it had suffered since the end of the Second World War. The other reason was the combination of nationalist excitement and poverty in certain of the regions involved.

In some cases no intervention was needed; in others it was rendered impracticable by geography or politics. In others again—Formosa, Lebanon, Jordan, and Aden—it was undertaken with good results by the United States and Britain. The critics were right in pointing out that *mobile* 'conventional' fighting power, founded on carriers, landing craft, highly trained troop contingents moved in aircraft both fast and of great capacity, together with the best possible organization of available bases, furnished the most promising means of imposing respect and of preventing or checking limited aggressions in remote areas. These represented the immediate risks of the period. The critics—and the planners—would be blind if they neglected them. What the former often failed to bear in mind was the background. The West would not dare to take action of any sort to stop even aggression of trifling extent if it faced nuclear weapons and possessed none itself. The deterrent does in fact deter.

The other measures called for do not come within the scope of this study. They are spiritual, economic, and political. The relief of misery, aid in the development of industry and communications to raise the standard of living, education and efforts to relax tension and negotiate a start in disarmament may represent the greatest and most beneficent tasks of all. They must be dealt with by other pens and in other works. All that can be done here is to advocate them and wish them well.

The final glance must be directed upon some general ideas concerned with both strategy and tactics. Let it be borne in mind that the orthodox is what the enemy almost always expects, so that it is from the first saddled with a heavy handicap. Perhaps it proves to be the only course possible or offers such vastly superior advantages that the commander cannot afford to set it aside. Even so, some variety or disguise can almost certainly be introduced into it by timing or feint. Otherwise the aim in war should constantly be to do what the enemy does not expect. Again, if it be considered that the search for the unexpected involves extra risks, as it frequently may, let it not be forgotten that it also provides compensations for them. It may not be possible to assess the compensations as closely as the risks, but there can be no doubt that they exist. The hostile commander suddenly begins to feel that he is being foxed. With modern means at his disposal for obtaining information he is unlikely to remain in the dark for long, but the briefest period of uncertainty may be priceless to his foe. It represents a plus to set against the minus represented by the risks taken. And this plus will often exceed the minus.

Then, let us remember that the terrific fire power of the troops of high-grade armies presents to the attacker, if his object has been divined and he is met by a prepared and reinforced defence, risks by comparison with which those of an unorthodox thrust are minor in character. There is a phrase much used by soldiers to describe the incorporeal obscurity which often shrouds the theatre of war or the battlefield: 'the fog of war'. But the reality from which the image is taken is also an element in war. The physical fog which is a product of the weather has again and again played its part, and the generally accepted verdict is that it favours the attack rather than the defence. Today artificial fog can be created over wide areas with the same result. So originality and unexpected action may be masked by three kinds of fog: the symbolic or metaphorical sort which hides what is 'on the other side of the hill'; the true fog created by nature; and the artificial fog created by the scientist and the military engineer. They are all the allies of the originally minded attacker and will not wholly desert him even when his action is marked by rashness. 'The most daring and even imprudent manœuvre has a good chance of success when the enemy is wondering what is happening.'[5]

Bourcet's dictum that every plan should have a second and even a third branch has been quoted.[6] It has a particular application to mountain warfare because in it the commander has to follow his luck to a great

[5] Falls, *Ordeal by Battle*, p. 47.
[6] See p. 29.

extent and may get through a pass which he expected
to be impregnable and be baulked at one through which
he hoped for an easy passage. Yet it is relevant to other
forms also, and today especially. In many wars of the
past, including the First World War, troops had to be
brought into such close contact with the enemy before
being launched to the attack that it was difficult to
make any subsequent alteration in their direction or
aim. Nowadays the head of a striking force may be
placed, let us say, forty miles from the front and
indeed many miles to a flank. This facilitates not only
surprise but flexibility, the ability to seize unexpected
opportunities, and the option of avoiding a hard
section of the enemy's front which was to have been
included in the assault. It does not do to cling too
pedantically or literally to the precept of 'maintenance of the aim'. As Captain Liddell Hart puts it, 'a
skilful opponent will choose a line that threatens
alternative objectives. And mechanized mobility will
give such an opponent the power to mask his direction
much longer than before, and to make a last-hour
swerve.'[7]

Deceive, mislead, confuse: this is the best recipe for
success. All very well for the theorist to talk, the
practical soldier may say, but the thing is not as easy
to do as it looks on paper and the atmosphere of the
battlefield has no resemblance to that of the study.
He is justified in the retort. Unless the theorist himself
has not only experienced war but seen with his own
eyes the commander's often agonizing struggle to

[7] Hart, *Dynamic Defence*, p. 60.

preserve control, to maintain movement, to repair mistakes and accidents, to make the dawdler remember the value of time, and above all to face within his own breast the sickening shock of the report of some local failure, perhaps involving in bloody loss troops whom he has intimately known and loved—unless the theorist can encompass all this and more, his ideas may be useful but the demands on leadership will elude him. It is the will to do what has to be done. This book is entitled *The Art of War* and ends with no intention on the part of its compiler of retreating from the implication of the name. It is, however, an art the pursuit of which is obstructed by constant collisions and frictions, moral, mental, and physical, such as no other activity described as an art experiences. 'The art of war,' said Napoleon at St. Helena, 'is a simple art; everything is in the performance.'

BOOK LIST

Army Air Forces in World War II. 7 Vols. Chicago: University Press.

Baxter, James Phinney: *The Introduction of the Ironclad Battleship.* Cambridge, Mass.: Harvard University Press.

Becke, Captain A. F.: *An Introduction to the History of Tactics, 1740–1905.* Hugh Rees.

Bourcet, Pierre de: *Principles de la guerre de montagnes.* Paris. (Privately printed by Ministère de la Guerre.)

Bryant, Arthur: *The Turn of the Tide.* Collins.

Bullock, Alan: *Hitler, A Study in Tyranny.* Odhams.

Callwell, Major-General C. E.: *Small Wars.* War Office.

Callwell, Major-General Sir Charles, and Headlam, Major-General Sir John: *The History of the Royal Artillery from the Indian Mutiny to the Great War.* 2 Vols. Woolwich. Royal Artillery Institution.

Carman, W. Y.: *A History of Firearms.* Routledge.

Clausewitz, Carl von: *On War.* 3 Vols. (Trans.) Kegan Paul.

Colin, Commandant: *The Transformations of War.* (Trans.).

Corbett, Julian S.: *Fighting Instructions, 1530–1816.* Navy Records Society, Vol. XXIX.

—— *Some Principles of Maritime Strategy.* Longmans.

Coupland, Sir Reginald: *Zulu Battle Piece.* Collins.

Creswell, Captain John: *Sea Warfare, 1939–1945.* Longmans.

Cuming, E. D. (Ed.): *Squire Osbaldeston, his Autobiography.* Lane.

De Gaulle, General: *The Edge of the Sword.* (Trans.) Faber & Faber.

Derrécagaix, General: *La Guerre moderne.* 2 Vols.

Domville-Fife, Charles: *Submarines and Sea Power.* Duckworth.

Douhet, Giulio: *The Command of the Air.* (Trans.). Faber & Faber.

Edmonds, Brig.-General Sir James: *A Short History of World War I.* Oxford: University Press.

Falls, Cyril: *A Hundred Years of War*. Duckworth.

—— *France and Belgium, 1917*. Vol. I. Macmillan.

—— *Mountjoy, Elizabethan General*. Odhams.

—— *Ordeal by Battle*. Methuen.

—— *The First World War*. Longmans.

—— *The Gordon Highlanders in the First World War*. Aberdeen: University Press.

—— *The Nature of Modern Warfare*. 2nd Ed. Methuen.

—— *The Second World War*. 3rd Ed. Methuen.

Fifteen Nations. No. 9/10. (N.A.T.O. Periodical).

Foch, Maréchal: *De la Conduite de la Guerre*. Paris: Berger-Levrault.

Fortescue, Sir John: *A History of the British Army*. Vol. XIII (1930).

Freeman, Douglas Southall: *R. E. Lee*. New York: 4 Vols. Scribner's Sons.

Fuller, Major-General J. F. C.: *The Decisive Battles of the Western World*. 3 Vols. Eyre & Spottiswoode.

—— *War and Western Civilisation*. Duckworth.

Guibert, Jacques-Antoine-Hypolite de: *Essai général de Tactique*. 2 Vols. Liège (1775).

—— *General Essay on Tactics*, (Trans.). London (1781).

Hart, B. H. Liddell: *Dynamic Defence*. Faber & Faber.

—— *The Ghost of Napoleon*. Faber & Faber.

—— *The Real War, 1914–1918*. Faber & Faber.

—— *The Tanks, The History of the Royal Tank Regiment*. 2 Vols. Cassell.

Herold, J. Christopher: *The Mind of Napoleon: A Selection from his Written and Spoken Words*. New York: Columbia University Press.

Hohenlohe-Ingelfingen, Prince Kraft zu: *Letters on Artillery*. (Trans.). Stanford.

Jones, H. A.: *The War in the Air*. 6 Vols. (Vol. I by Sir Walter Raleigh.) Oxford: Clarendon Press. (1922 &c.)

Kessel, Eberhard: *Generalfeldmarschall Graf Alfred Schlieffen. Briefe*. Göttingen: Vandenhoeck & Ruprecht.

Lloyd, Christopher: *The Keith Papers*. Vol. II. Navy Records Society. Vol. XC.

Luard, Captain C. E.: *Field Railways and their General Application in War*. Journal of the Royal United Service Institution. Vol. XVII. (1874)

Mahan, Captain A. T.: *The Life of Nelson*. 2nd Ed. Sampson Low.

Manstein, Field-Marshal Erich von: *Lost Victories*. (Trans.) Methuen.

Maurice, Lieutenant F.: *The System of Field Manoeuvres*. Blackwood (1872).

Mellenthin, Major-General F. W. von: *Panzer Battles, 1939–1945*. (Trans.) Cassell.

Montgomery: *The Memoirs of Field-Marshal the Viscount Montgomery*. Collins.

Morison, Samuel Eliot: *History of United States Naval Operations in World War II* (general title):
—— *New Guinea and the Marianas*. Oxford: University Press.
—— *The Battle of the Atlantic*. Oxford: University Press.
—— *The Rising Sun in the Pacific*. Oxford: University Press.
—— *The Struggle for Guadalcanal*. Oxford: University Press.

Oman, Sir Charles: *Studies in the Napoleonic Wars*. Methuen.

Oppenheim: *International Law*. 6th Ed. Longmans.

Parkes, Oscar: *British Battleships, Warrior 1860 to Vanguard 1950*. Seely Service.

Playfair, Major-General I. S. O., and Others. *The Mediterranean and Middle East*. Vol. I. H.M. Stationery Office (1954).

Preston, Richard A., Wise, Sidney F., & Werner, Herman O. *Men in Arms, A History of Warfare and its Interrelationships with Western Society*. Atlantic Press.

Quimby, Robert S.: *The Background of Napoleonic Warfare, The Theory of Military Tactics in Eighteenth-Century France*. New York: Columbia University Press.

Rand Corporation: *Report of a Study of Non-Military Defense* (privately printed).

Rawlins, Colonel S. W. H.: *A History of the Development of the English Artillery in France*. (War Office MS., 1919).

Regele, Oskar: *Feldmarschall Radetzky*. Vienna & Munich: Herold.

Ritter, Gerhard: *The Schlieffen Plan, Critique of a Myth*. (Trans.) Wolff.

Roskill, Captain S. W.: *The War at Sea*. Vols. I & II. H.M. Stationery Office.

Rowe, Vivian: *The Great Wall of France, The Triumph of the Maginot Line*. Putnam.

Salter, J. A.: *Allied Shipping Control*. Oxford: Clarendon Press.

Slessor, Marshal of the Royal Air Force Sir John: *Strategy for the West*. Cassell.

—— *The Central Blue*. Cassell.

Smyth, Brigadier Sir John: *The Only Enemy*. Hutchinson.

Sydenham Clarke, Sir George: *Fortifications*.

Westphal, Lieut.-General Siegfried, and Others: *The Fatal Decisions*. Michael Joseph.

Wilkinson, Spenser: *The Command of the Sea and the Brain of the Navy*. Constable.

—— *The French Army before Napoleon*. Oxford: Clarendon Press.

—— *The Rise of General Bonaparte*. Oxford: Clarendon Press.

Willoughby, Major-General Charles A., and Chamberlain, John: *MacArthur, 1941–1951: Victory in the Pacific*. Heinemann.

The place of publication is always London unless otherwise stated.

INDEX

Dates of monarchs are those of the years during which they reigned; dates of other persons are those of birth and death.

HESPERIDES BOOKS
